TEMPLE
Grandin

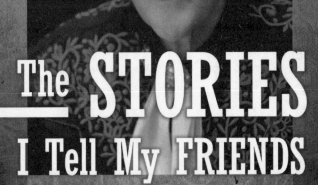

The STORIES
I Tell My FRIENDS

by Anita Lesko

Foreword by Mick Jackson
Emmy Award-winning director of
the HBO Movie *Temple Grandin*

Advance Praise for *The Stories I Tell My Friends*

"Anita Lesko has given us a rare inside view of what makes our hero Temple Grandin tick. A must-read!"

— **Joanne Lara**
Autism Movement Therapy &
Autism Works Now

"Temple Grandin has been a wonderful trailblazer for everyone impacted by autism. Anita Lesko's book on Temple is a must-read for people who want to understand and accept those with autism. Anita's writings and daily work make her an ideal author for this important book."

— **Scott Badesch**
President/CEO
Autism Society of America
Bethesda, MD

TEMPLE GRANDIN – THE STORIES I TELL MY FRIENDS

All marketing and publishing rights guaranteed to and reserved by:

FUTURE HORIZONS INC.

721 W. Abram Street
Arlington, TX 76013
(800) 489-0727
(817) 277-0727
(817) 277-2270 (fax)
E-mail: info@fhautism.com
www.fhautism.com

Cover & interior design by John Yacio III

ISBN: 9781941765609

DEDICATION

I dedicate this book to every single person on the autism spectrum. It is my hope that this book changes the world's view of autism. It will be a much better place for all of us.

— **Anita Lesko**

CONTENTS

Contents

FOREWORD

by Mick Jackson

It isn't at all easy to describe Temple Grandin to someone who hasn't heard of her, or who doesn't know anything about her, her life, or her career. Where would you start? Where would you stop? The world that Temple inhabits is complex and surprising and multi-faceted in a way that defies any easy summarization. As does Temple herself. And, in the world of Hollywood movie pitches, for example, if you were trying to enthuse some unaware studio executive with the idea of telling her life story, there isn't an immediately promising "log-line" that you could start with. ("I have a great movie idea for you!" "What's it about?" "It's about a woman with autism who designs slaughterhouses." "Oh.")

Fortunately, there were people at HBO Films who did want to know more and who, in 2010, eventually green-lighted a movie about her extraordinary life. I was the lucky director given the task of directing it and telling her story, and that is how I got to find out about and meet this remarkable woman. Now, through the somewhat unexpected success of that movie and through Temple's many books about herself and her work, many more people have found a source of great inspiration, hope, and joy in her storied career and her struggles.

And yet, in the wildly heterogeneous universe that is Temple, there is always more to discover.

In this delightful book, Anita Lesko has had the happy idea of letting Temple and many of the people in her life, including her students, sit down and tell stories—stories not just about her and her life, but how their own lives were changed by her. In a refreshingly direct and breezy conversational style, Ms. Lesko patiently listens and probes. If the questions are particularly relevant, this is because Anita herself has autism, diagnosed late in life, and has shared many of the same struggles and personal triumphs as her subject. She makes an empathetic and engaged interviewer.

What comes through most strikingly in these stories is a great sense of both fun and purpose. Through all the tales of hardship, misunderstanding, prejudice, and bullying, Temple's wit and humor shine through, often with a child-like glee in the telling of the details. If many of the difficulties and hardships she encountered seem cruel and overwhelming, they are mastered and ultimately surmounted by sheer force of will and perseverance. Temple tells, with passion, of forcing herself as a child to learn how to do the things that were most difficult, over and over, until the fear of them lost its power. In this, she had the support and encouragement of her mother and others close to her. Her advice to parents of children with autism spectrum disorders like her own is simple and direct: "Push them out into the world. Get them out doing things, even if they are hard. Don't leave them isolated indoors with a TV or lap-top. You get better and better by getting out there and doing stuff. You learn everything by doing."

Reading the accounts of those who shared Temple's brave encounters with the world, her sense of achievement in seeing things that others failed to notice, her greater and greater contribution to our understanding of animal welfare, and her fierce mission to explain and

Foreword

to teach her students, one is aware, not just of the love and admiration she generates in everyone who comes into contact with her, but their sense of awe, too. Her pioneering achievements in animal science and her determination to engage with the world on her own terms—despite all odds—are indeed awesome.

In 2010, *Time* magazine included Temple in its list of the 100 Most Influential People in the World. Reading these stories that Anita Lesko has put together so well, you can see why. And you can certainly sense that awe, too.

— **Mick Jackson**
Pacific Palisades, California
November 2017

■ INTRODUCTION ■

by Temple Grandin

My Friend Anita Lesko

I'd like you to meet my friend, Anita. She was the perfect person to write this book. Her path to a successful career was similar to mine, but had some important differences, too. This background, along with our many conversations, gives her a great perspective for telling this story. Anita was diagnosed with autism later in life—she always knew she was different, but she didn't know why. Growing up in a family with little money presented many obstacles for her to overcome. Today, through hard work and perseverance, she is a successful nurse anesthetist. She is the doctor's choice for anesthesia when there is a complex brain surgery; they want her because she is the best!

Both Anita and I love horses. As a teenager, she cleaned stalls for riding lessons. We both learned the value of hard work in the horse barn. Anita advanced all the way to show jumping; a great example that hard work and perseverance lead to meeting your goals.

Her next job, a concession stand at an ice arena, taught her how to talk to people. Restless, she wanted to perform more exciting jobs. She learned how to operate the spotlights, and after a lot of pestering of the management, got to drive the Zamboni. Late at night, Anita got free skating practice time on the rink. Anita and I were both expert finders of the "back door" into many successful pursuits. I painted signs for local businesses and did carpentry work. Freelance sign painting morphed into designing livestock corrals. I started my business one small project at a time, and so did she.

Anita has so much to be proud of, such as paying off student loans and medical expenses for her parents. For years, half her nurse anesthetist salary went to paying back all her loans. Today, they are fully paid. She married an Aspie after learning she's on the autism spectrum, presenting a great example that people on the spectrum can and do form deep relationships. Her next goal is to teach others how to be a nurse anesthetist.

So many of Anita's qualities make her a great careerwoman and author, but also an excellent friend. I have enjoyed working with her on her journey to create this book, and I would choose no one else to tell you the stories in these pages aside from my friend, Anita Lesko.

— **Temple Grandin, Professor**
Department of Animal Science
Colorado State University

■ INTRODUCTION ■

by Anita Lesko

Hero. According to the Merriam-Webster dictionary, the definition of a hero is:

  A: a mythological or legendary figure endowed with great strength or ability

  B: an illustrious warrior (illustrious- notably or brilliantly outstanding because of dignity or achievements or actions)

  C: a person admired for achievements and noble qualities

  D: one who shows great courage

There is one person who immediately comes to mind when I read the definition of the word *hero*: Temple Grandin. Her qualities far exceed the definition above—it would have to include: philanthropist, humanitarian, revered, strong integrity, honest, selfless, loyal, trustworthy, humble, and so much more.

On March 28, 2017 I had the distinct honor to speak at the United Nations Headquarters for World Autism Awareness Day. I have autism, diagnosed at age fifty. During my presentation, in referring to individuals with autism, I used the idiom "still water runs deep." I talked about how individuals with autism might not show it on the surface, but there's a lot of emotion going on inside. Temple is just like the rest of us in this regard. She might not necessarily demonstrate it with facial expressions, but her emotions and passions run the depth of the deepest oceans.

I am a good friend of Temple's, and this book was born from that relationship. I first met Temple back in 2011 when she contacted me asking permission to include me in a new book she was working on, *Different … Not Less.* I am featured in Chapter Seven: "Nurse Anesthetist/Military Aviation Photojournalist." We would periodically talk on the phone, and the conversation would always contain the topic of working and jobs. In 2013, I had organized an autism conference and invited Temple to be the keynote speaker. That was when I finally met her in person. We continued with phone calls every now and then, just to say hello and see how the other was doing.

One day back in early March 2017, I called Temple just to say hi. She was at an airport, and early into the conversation a door alarm suddenly started sounding right nearby where Temple was sitting. Temple blurted out, "Good grief! A door alarm just went off! I've got to get off the phone!" She obviously couldn't continue the conversation, so the call was quickly ended. The next day I was at work when she called me back. Fortunately, I was between cases and had a bit of time to chat. "Hi, Anita, it's Temple Grandin." I always get a kick out of it when she says her last name. How many people do you know named Temple? Temple was in good form, and was telling me something she found extremely entertaining. She got into quite the laughing spell and inflicted it onto me, so we were both laughing heartily! After we said goodbye, I lingered where I was, resting my elbows on the window sill in the hallway of the operating room and gazing out at the rainy day. As I turned to go back to my room and get ready for the next case, I was

Introduction

chuckling to myself as I reminisced our fun conversation. I wished the rest of the world could see that part of Temple, the "real person" side of her. Suddenly, it hit me. The entire world could get to see Temple like they've never seen her before; I could write a book about her! I knew other books have been written about Temple, but this one would be very different. This would be a person with autism writing about another person with autism. We have a lot in common. In fact, in the afterword, I'll share with you my personal discovery that resulted from this incredible journey.

Later that afternoon, I called Temple to ask her what she thought about me writing a book about her. She loved the idea! I sent an email to Teresa Corey, Temple's liaison, to toss the idea at her, too. She reminded me that there are already several biographies about Temple, and proceeded to suggest a book collecting Temples memoirs, all her antics, and stories she shares with those closest to her. I was thrilled, and my mind was already churning with ideas.

When I first set out to begin interviewing Temple, I thought it would only entail the conversations she and I had, but this experience unfolded into something far greater than I ever expected, and revealed things about Temple that no one knows. Opportunities arose which enabled me to meet the famous Emmy Award-winning Hollywood director, Mick Jackson, who directed the HBO movie *Temple Grandin*. I got to meet Temple's present and former graduate students, and get their thoughts and feelings about Temple and the impact she had on their lives. I had the pleasure of meeting those people closest to Temple, with whom she's been friends for decades. I was present at her seventieth birthday celebration at Colorado State University, when she revealed that she's fully funded eighteen graduate students to date. I rode with her in her SUV from the CSU campus out to the farm where she teaches her students the cattle handing skills she's mastered. I've seen Temple speak at autism conferences, but getting to see her working the cattle was a highlight of my life. She was in her element. I had the opportunity to speak with Jim Uhl, a key person in Temple's life, who she met just after graduating from Arizona State University. It's been a wild and exciting ride!

Throughout the pages of this book, you will get to know Temple like you've never seen her. I've got some news that will knock your socks off—Temple has been sharing stories with me that she's never told anyone. You'll hear about one of her great passions, the National Aeronautics and Space Administration (NASA), astronauts, and even how the Playtex company is involved in it all. You will find out her deepest thoughts, what makes her cry, her happiest memories, and her biggest dreams. Everything is in her own words, from her childhood Christmas memories, to the most thrilling thing she's ever done. All our conversations were recorded, as I didn't want to miss a single word, so everything is written like Temple said it.

When you are around Temple, you are guaranteed to learn something new each day—probably more than one thing! After each time we'd talk, there would typically be several things she mentioned that I had to look up online. I've learned a lot, not only about her life, but

Introduction

about life in general. Temple is like a walking search engine; she reads constantly, keeps up-to-date on world affairs, technology, and simply everything. She would make an excellent world news correspondent. She mentioned that at every airport she's at, which is multiple times per week, she heads to whatever shop she can find that sells magazines, newspapers, and books, and loads up on all the educational material to read on the plane. When was the last time you purchased a *New York Times*, *Wall Street Journal*, *Wired*, and *Discover*, just to read in your spare time? Temple doesn't leave any stone unturned: she's a human dynamo, and a tough act to follow! Does she ever focus on the fact that she has autism? Hardly. She truly has broken all the barriers in that aspect, and getting to know her should inspire everyone on the autism spectrum to not focus on the autism, but instead focus on new goals you set for yourself, and follow your passions and dreams.

I'm the luckiest person on Earth to know Temple so well. She gave me permission to write this tell-all book about her, so by the time you're finishing up the last page, you will feel like Temple is your friend, too. As you learn about Temple as a person, you'll be shocked, surprised, delighted, and inspired. Her many facets reach far beyond what anyone has ever seen.

The purpose of this book goes beyond getting to know just how great Temple Grandin is. It serves to show the world how truly human an individual with autism can be. I want it to break down all barriers for individuals with autism, as this proves the depth of emotion and passion that lies beneath the surface of autism. Temple's wish is that it serves to inspire everyone with autism to get out there and "just do" the things they aspire to; she wants everyone to enjoy life and be successful, in whatever they choose to do!

If everyone (not just those on the autism spectrum) lived their life like Temple does, the world would be a much better place. She maintains the highest level of integrity I have ever seen. She says it's her responsibility to be the best role model possible, as she knows that millions of people look up to her. She's always on her best behavior, as she is recognized wherever she goes. Temple is always happy to pose for photos, sign autographs, respond to fan mail with handwritten letters, and even take calls from fans. She's world-famous, but you'd never know it when you are around her. She's humble and talks to everyone with the same level of respect. She takes it all in stride.

It's time now to come along with me on this adventure and get to know your new friend, Temple Grandin!

— **Anita Lesko**

CHAPTER 1
Filming of the HBO Movie
Temple Grandin

L ights! Camera! Action!

On February 6, 2010 the HBO movie *Temple Grandin* made its debut to the whole world. From that moment, Dr. Temple Grandin went from being well-known to a global phenomenon. It was not just the autism world and the meat industry any more, everyone was taken by Temple's fascinating life. The movie, directed by Mick Jackson (multiple award-winning British film director and television producer), made a historic impact for autism that changed millions of lives. It shows that through mentoring and sheer will, Temple, a young woman with autism, succeeds against all odds. The Emmy Award-winning movie, starring Claire Danes as Temple Grandin, brought autism into the spotlight. One of the many things it did was give parents a look into the mind of their children with autism, enabling them to finally understand how they experience the world.

Temple's Birthday Bash

Temple invited me to her big birthday celebration on August 29, 2017 to be held at Colorado State University. I was thrilled when I received the invitation, which was sent by Teresa Corey, Temple's liaison. The second I read it, I was on the phone with the recommended hotel. As soon as I made reservations for our room, the next call was to book our flights. Soon, everything was all set for the trip.

Fortunately, I was able to get the necessary time off from my work as an anesthetist to fly out to Fort Collins, Colorado. My husband Abraham, who also has autism, took a brief leave of absence from his job to accompany me on this adventurous journey. Our "daughter," Callie Mae (the cat who lost her legs), would be coming along as well—as she always did on the trips we make.

It was Tuesday, August 29th and there I was at Temple's big birthday bash. I was sitting at a table under a huge tent along with Teresa Corey, Jennifer Gilpin Yacio, and Brad Masella, all from Future Horizons. There was music playing from the seventies, accompanied by an announcement that Temple had requested that genre, and that it was hoped that everyone is enjoying the music. If not, then take it up with Temple! There were huge round tables set up, enough for several hundred people to be seated. Each table was covered in crisp white linen table cloths, adorned by custom crafted centerpieces: handcrafted pine boxes with greenery and yellow marigolds in them, branded on the outside with "CSU" for Colorado State University and "TG" for Temple Grandin. It was announced that the branding of the boxes was performed in a humane fashion, which garnered much laughter from the lively crowd. There was a long table set up through the middle of the tent, which would hold the delicious food soon to be set up. The entire venue was set on the luxurious lawn directly in front of the

Chapter 1

Animal Sciences building on the CSU campus. That building is home to Temple's office, where everyone knows her and she has spent many years of her life.

I was sipping on my ice water when Teresa leaned against my shoulder, whispering as she motioned with her head, "There's Mick Jackson, the guy who directed Temple's movie." I slowly turned around to see who she was motioning at. "The man with the white hat," Teresa stated. Yes, there he was, sporting his white hat. Even if Teresa had not said a word, I would have sensed there was something unique about him. Indeed, there was, as I'd soon find out. Nudging me, Teresa then prompted, "Why don't you go over to him? Tell him you're Temple's friend, that you are writing a book about her, and you'd like to interview him!" Without batting an eye, I was getting up from my seat and making my way through the crowd to get to him.

There happened to be an empty seat right next to Mick, so I boldly sat down. He was talking to someone when I first arrived. Once done he turned to me, sensing I'd come there seeking his attention. He smiled warmly at me, giving me a calm feeling. I repeated Teresa's words, "Hi! I'm a friend of Temple, and I'm writing a book about her! I'd like to interview you at a later time." I held my breath for a moment, wondering what his reply would be. Smiling, Mick quickly responded, "Why, yes of course. I'd be happy to talk with you!" He reached for a napkin, pulled a pen out of his pocket, and wrote his name and number on it. Smiling, he nodded his head toward the napkin and commented, "I used a lot of napkins to draw out scenes for the cast and crew while working on Temple's movie." He completed writing his information on the napkin, then handed it to me. I very carefully folded it, placing it deeply in my shirt pocket and fastening the snap to ensure I wouldn't lose that precious data. I was quite beside myself that I'd get to include the director of Temple's world-famous movie in my book!

Mick leaned towards me and prompted, "So, tell me about yourself." I proceeded, "I also have autism, diagnosed at age fifty." I went on to tell him that I've been a nurse anesthetist for the past thirty years, and that I have a new book coming out about autism and health care. I then thanked Mick for his number, to which he responded, "I'm looking forward to hearing from you!" I got up from my seat and returned to my table, collapsing in the chair next to Teresa and gushing, "I'm so excited! Mick just gave me his phone number and said he's looking forward to hearing from me." Teresa replied, "Wow! That's great! See, aren't you glad you went over to him?" Indeed, I was.

Several days later, once back home, I figured I'd wait yet a few more days before calling Mick for his interview. I wanted to be sure he was back home and rested. Finally, the day came that I decided to call him. Tape recorder all set and rolling, I dialed the number he had neatly written on the napkin. After several rings he answered, quickly remembering who I was.

The first question I asked him was, "What was your first impression of Temple when you finally met her?" Mick began, "I knew exactly what to expect because I'd already read her books, and things written about her by Oliver Sacks. Also, the script screenwriter, Christopher

Chapter 1

Monger, had been to see her and filled me in. I found her to be very open, very charming, and surprisingly witty! I'm not sure how much she intended to be witty … she's a very lovely person. She could not have been nicer."

Mick continued, "The more I got to know her, the more I thought she would have made a good director, because of her amazing powers of observation. That's what directing is all about. She has that amazing ability to see things that others don't see. I love that story she told during her birthday celebration about being the only one who saw the eclipse coming through the leaves on the tree onto the sidewalk, as if there were a thousand pinhole cameras showing the eclipse. A director would have seen something like that. And actually, I hadn't even realized it until we had finished the film—and I had worked a lot with her on it, as she occasionally came to the set to observe what was going on."

I was intently listening to Mick's every word. "One time, she came to the set of what was meant to be her dorm room. I had no idea what it had actually looked like, aside from what she had told me and what I read in her books. We had the stage set up to reflect how I thought it would have looked. I said, 'Temple, I know this is not what your room actually looked like,' to which she responded, 'No, but it could have been.'" Mick continued, "I thought this was remarkably sophisticated for her to say, as that's what films do. Others might have said no, it was nothing like that, but instead, she simply looked around and stated, yes, it could easily have been just like that."

Mick continued, "When the film was complete, we invited her to come and watch it in a screening room. All the executives from HBO were there, very much wanting to know what Temple's reaction would be to the film. So finally, at the end of the film when all the credits ran, we were all sitting there, and everybody is sort of trying not to look at Temple, who wasn't saying anything. Obviously, she was processing the film, not realizing that people were expecting her to speak. I was sitting next to her, so I leaned over and said, 'Temple, I think people would like to know what you think of the film.' She blurted out in a loud excited tone, 'I think it's fantastic! I think it's fantastic!'"

It wasn't until a little while later when Mick discovered what the visual thinking portrayed in the movie truly meant. Mick went on, "What I hadn't realized until afterwards, after she shook everyone's hand then left to where she was staying, was ..." He seemed to drift out of this thought, and began to tell it another way. "I was driving home in my car and my phone rang. It was Temple, and she couldn't stop talking about the film. She was going on in all sorts of directions, and it was apparent that she absorbed every detail of the film into her head and she was running it as she was talking to me. I portrayed that in the movie, but in that moment, I realized it was actually true; she was able to amazingly take on a huge amount of information, and just store it in her head. She said it's like a movie running in her head, and she can play it, fast forward, freeze it, everything. That was a shockingly impressive look inside how her mind works."

Chapter 1

I could tell throughout the conversation how pleased Mick was with Temple and her input. Mick said, "Temple was really helpful throughout the shooting of the film, especially to Claire Danes. I don't know if you know this, but before the filming began, Claire invited Temple to her and her fiancé's apartment in New York City. Temple spent the whole afternoon there, with a video camera running on her the entire time. Claire's fiancé is also an actor, and has played characters with autism. While he operated the camera, Claire noted the way Temple talked, the way she walked, the way she talked about things that were important to her, and kept the video of all that. Then, every day on the set when we were about to shoot a scene, Claire Danes would go off into a quiet corner and look at the video again to listen to her words and get Temple inside her head. To the people on the set who knew Temple, they were amazed at how Claire acted just like her, as if she channeled Temple through her." I remember Temple telling me how she was astounded the way Claire Danes became her. A bit later, I'll also share what Temple noticed when she walked into Claire's apartment—just reminiscing about it sent Temple into hearty laughter!

Mick seemed genuinely thrilled that Temple gave him a big hug. He shared this, "At the end of the production, when we were about to go back and edit the movie, Temple actually gave Claire and me a hug. I know that it's easier for her to give hugs now, but back then it was very difficult for her to give hugs (which is why she built a squeeze machine). Everyone wanted to hug her at the end of the filming because she was so genuine and open. I think she realized that, and she hugged

Claire, then she hugged me. I think that must have taken a great deal of emotional energy to do, but she did it. And that is a hug I shall certainly treasure the rest of my life."

That red squeeze machine from so long ago wasn't needed any longer.

Mick continued, "I think Temple was determined to have everything done just right. When she visited the set, she'd ask many questions and draw lots of pictures on napkins to show what she meant and to be sure we would show it exactly how she wanted it. Take, for example, the automatic gate at her aunt's ranch that she designed and built. We had to construct that gate, an exact replica of it, and know what the principles really were. So, Temple sat down with me while we were having coffee in a café, pulled out a napkin and a pen, drew it in great detail, and explained to me exactly how it worked." I thought back to the evening at Temple's seventieth birthday bash when Mick wrote on that napkin. I could tell he was used to using napkins as a good drawing board.

I was enjoying this immensely, listening to Mick. He went on, "When I was scouting for locations of the movie, I went back to her aunt's ranch where she had gone as a young girl, just to see what it looked like. There were people there, and they had no idea that it was Temple's aunt's ranch. I asked if they'd mind if I just walked around. So, I began walking around the corrals and things, and in the bushes was this red thing that caught my attention. It was the original squeeze chute! It was still there on the ranch. I pulled the branches away from

Chapter 1

it and found that on the bottom, 'TG Enterprises' was painted where she had signed it like an autograph. The people living there at the ranch had no idea it was still there or what it was. At that moment, we knew exactly what we were going to build for the film." Temple was a bit surprised when I shared with her later that Mick had gone back there, as Mick didn't tell her.

Very sincerely Mick stated, "She was so terribly generous with her time with Claire, Christopher, and me. She had many anecdotes to share, and what they meant to her, so we used them while creating the script. She'd describe all the images coming up in her head, like going to an online search engine, and all the images coming up at once. This was something a film could do, especially with someone like Temple. Not only can you show all the connections she makes between things, but how extraordinarily painful and difficult her life must have been for her. With sensory processing disorders, everything comes at you with double hurricane-force intensity; a pin dropping sounds like someone dropping a steel girder, or somebody coughing sounds the roaring of a lion. Sight, sound, and touch just comes at you with a hypersensitivity, like walking across a battlefield with bombs going off all around you. I don't think people understand that about people with autism, why they shrink from the world because it's so painful for them. When Temple seemed absent from the world, she was really just focused with a laser intensity on watching a cow do something, or watching the way a gate opened or closed." It was very obvious to me that Mick really understood what it's like to have autism and live in this world.

TEMPLE GRANDIN – The Stories I Tell My Friends

Mick continued with his thoughts about Temple, "I really enjoyed working with her, it was one of the greatest privileges of my life to have done that. It was one of the best films I've ever made because of her. We all loved her. She's a difficult person in some ways, but not by being unkind, and she can't help it, but just because she sees the world differently than others and doesn't react the same ways that others would. To see her in an airport terminal where people are recognizing her, and her reactions to all that attention is simply amazing. Knowing that she started out as this child with autism, and now is a superstar, is just amazing! I was talking to someone on the plane about her, and telling them that she was in *Time* magazine as one of the one hundred most influential people of this century. That's just astonishing, considering where her story started out."

"Yes, indeed, it is amazing," I agreed.

Mick continued, "That's what I can tell you from my experience with Temple during the filming of the movie, and immediately afterwards. I think she was both flattered and amazed that we were trying to recreate the moments of her life, like when we created the angles of that strange room at her school. Through this window, it appears to people looking in that a person changes in size when moving from one corner to another. It looks like small people become giant people, and giant people become small people as they walk by. We built that full-scale, and that was the first thing that we shot with her, and the first thing that's in the film: Temple walking into that room. We tried to capture the gentleness of her, too, particularly those scenes in the movie where she's with the animals. She puts her hand up to the side of the cattle and feels its beating heart. She has no fear of the horse that's dangerous in the paddock, only concern that the horse is feeling pain and she wants to calm it. The movie shows that individuals with autism can lead normal lives, in fact super normal lives, and can offer guidance to others for certain things, like how to properly treat cattle."

I stated, "Yes, that movie inspired millions of people, especially parents of children with autism, as well as individuals with autism themselves."

Mick then asked me about myself, and having autism. I began, "I think I mentioned to you that I didn't learn that I'm on the autism spectrum until I was fifty. I never knew why I was different and never fit in. Despite that, it never kept me from pursuing my goals." I told him I graduated from Columbia University in 1988 with my master's in nurse anesthesia, and I've been working full-time ever since as a certified registered nurse anesthetist. Mick piped in, "Wow! That's truly amazing! You have quite an impressive life yourself!" I proceeded to tell him, "I got to fly in an F-15 fighter jet when I became an internationally published military aviation photojournalist." Mick was duly impressed, and said, "You and Temple are very much alike! You are the perfect person to write this book!"

A Movie Like a Sixties and Seventies Time Machine

After talking to Mick about the movie, I wanted to get Temple's perspective about it. In our next phone conversation, I told her that I just spoke with Mick Jackson, and Temple was very pleased about that. I asked, "Temple, how did you feel when you watched the whole movie, when it was all done?" Temple's response was, "It was like going in a sixties and seventies time machine. It was really weird. She (Claire Danes) became me. And seeing the dip vat built and perfectly working! They did such a great job of it." I stated, "Mick told me how you went to New York City to meet with Claire Danes, and how you were filmed for four hours. Talk about that. What was it like to meet her?" Temple replied, "Well, most people are awestruck by movie stars. Claire was so much younger than I was, so it was almost like talking to a student. She just had a video camera set up, so we kind of forget about it. I talked a lot about anxiety, about what it was like to live with it, what visual thinking was like. That went on for about four hours. I spent more time with Mick Jackson and the writers than I did with Claire. When I worked on the dip vat down on the movie site, it was like I traveled back to the seventies at a real job site. I was there with a real welder. The scene took place at Capitol Land and Cattle Company in San Antonio, Texas. They had all the cattle right there, and they built the dip vat right there. I had to make sure it was properly functioning, so no cattle would drown or anything."

"Right," I stated, "that would not have been a good thing."

I told Temple that Mick had gone to visit the ranch her aunt had owned, and discovered the original red squeeze chute, which was used by the cowboys on the ranch for holding anxious cattle still while they were being inoculated, in some brush. Temple didn't know that Mick

Chapter 1

had gone there, and found that a bit surprising. "Mick was absolutely the right person to do this movie," Temple stated. I asked Temple how long it had taken to actually make the movie. "Well," she responded, "once they got Mick Jackson to do the movie, it didn't take that long. There had been two other teams that didn't work out. But once they got Mick, it went pretty quickly. Mick chose all the acting crew, as well. He chose Claire Danes because he'd seen her play the part of Christina ... you know, that famous painting by Andrew Wyeth, *Christina's World*. Mick Jackson is a visual thinker, and he really got it."

I told Temple what Mick had said to me about her reaction to the completed film. "Mick talked about the day you came for the showing of the completed film. He was worried when you just sat there without saying anything. Then finally, he asked you how you liked it." Here's what Temple reminisced, "Well, I was sitting there watching it and getting my mind blown, and that's why I wasn't saying anything!" She went on, "It was just overwhelming to sit there and watch my life's story unfold on the screen." I replied, "Well sure, I can imagine how overwhelming it was for you!"

"Here's a question for you, Temple," I continued, "what was the message you hoped everyone who saw the movie would take away from it?" Temple gave me her answer, "I've had a lot of kids write to me and say I inspired them to be successful. That's really important. And I've had women in engineering come up to me and say that the movie inspired them to stick it out and get their degree in engineering. I liked how the movie showed my aunt Ann, my mother, and science teacher really well. But I really liked that it showed my projects, and it also showed how visual thinking works. It makes people understand visual thinking. Mick Jackson is a visual thinker."

I had heard Mick Jackson's thoughts about when he first met Temple, and I wanted to know what Temple thought when she first met Mick. "So, Temple," I inquired, "what was your first impression of Mick when you met him?" Temple went on, "Well, I remember meeting him in a restaurant, and we were going to have either lunch or dinner, and he couldn't eat. I said, 'Mick, aren't you going to get something to eat?' He said he had a problem, and if he had something to eat he'd be sick all day; he had gotten sick from something in Morocco. I thought, 'Man, that's got to be miserable.' So here I am, ordering food and eating in a restaurant, and he's not eating. I felt really bad eating in front of him, but I was really hungry. If I don't eat something, I get a headache. I can't really remember everything we talked about. I talked about visual thinking, stuff I built. The thing that I noticed about Mick was that I'd say something very casually to him, and it would end up in the movie! When I talked to him about it, it didn't seem to register that much."

Thinking back to my conversation with Mick, I remembered him telling me about the moment he truly understood how Temple's mind worked. "Temple, Mick told me about the moment when you called him while he was driving, when he truly realized your visual thinking." Temple's tone had excitement in it as she replied, "Well, it was like going back to the sixties and seventies, it was really trippy, and I didn't have much to say about it the moment I first watched it. I had

Chapter 1

to play it back in my head. Sometimes with movies, I enjoy them more when I replay them in my head." I understood exactly what she was saying, and piped up, "You sort of process it better and more deeply afterwards." Temple agreed, "Right, that's what I did." I've always done this, and now I learned Temple does it, as well. I wondered if everyone does it, or just those with visual thinking.

I was quite curious to hear what Temple thought of Claire Danes when she went to Claire's apartment in New York City for their first meeting. "I've got some questions for you about Claire Danes. What did you first think of her when you got to her apartment in New York City?" I smiled at Temple's response. Temple gushed, "She had a really nice apartment, with this really weird stuff right in the front foyer. It was a big red thing that looked like a giant red cow plop! (Temple started giggling quite profusely as she shared this with me.) And above it was a sort of abstract art of a clown, and I'm thinking, 'That's a weird kind of decoration!' I think I did ask her about it. Then, we sat down at the kitchen table, and there was another person there with her. We talked for about four hours, then we went out for lunch to a restaurant. I can remember walking out to the street with her, and we talked about how visual thinking worked. She videotaped our whole meeting so she'd have that to study. And then I gave her an ancient old Larry King tape from 1988. At first, I thought it would be hard for her to become me, but she did! She seemed really, really serious about what she was doing."

I knew that Mr. Carlock, Temple's science teacher at the Hampshire boarding school, was a pivotal person in her life. He recognized

Temple's potential and took her under his wing, and he challenged her with special projects that encouraged her to solve them. The movie did an excellent job of sharing that with the audience. I wanted to hear how seeing him portrayed affected Temple. I already knew the response I was about to hear when I asked Temple, "What kind of emotions were stirred up inside you when you saw David Strathairn playing the part of Mr. Carlock? How did it make you feel?" Temple's voice got strained, and I could tell she was getting choked up. "Well, I saw the picture with the NASA astronaut, David Strathairn, holding the helmet, and I broke down into tears. I just broke down and cried about that." I heard though the phone that Temple was crying, so I remained silent and waited until she was ready to continue. I knew she was playing those scenes with him in the movie in her mind. Finally, she went on, "It was a real astronaut helmet he was holding. Then, when I looked at the rocket they had, I thought that it didn't look balanced, and that perhaps they didn't do a weight and balance. When I talked to the stage hand, it turned out they hadn't. I noticed that in the movie." At this point I started chuckling to myself, as Temple's logical side was back in order. She continued, "The other thing that was really weird, was when we went to a filming in New York, and Catherine O'Hara and David Strathairn were there, and Catherine O'Hara was sitting near me, and it was like having my aunt Ann there. I know that's totally weird, but that's how it felt. She really looked and acted like Ann. I told her she did a great job."

Chapter 1

The Happiest Part of the Movie

I wanted to know what made Temple the happiest when she watched the movie. Can you guess what it was? I didn't guess correctly! Here's what Temple got just tickled over. "So, Temple," I asked, "what made you the happiest when you saw the film?" Temple replied, "Watching the dip vat working! That was happy! My actual drawings were in the movie. They took really great shots of the dip vat from a cherry picker; it was really high and scary, but they got some really beautiful shots. Seeing my projects really excited me!" I was envisioning the big grin on her face on the other end of the call. I know her very well and the facial expressions she makes, and how gleeful she gets at things. This surely was one of them.

Of course, if there's a movie made about anyone's life, there are going to be parts that are sad and might bring great pain. It would certainly transport you back to that place, where you relive it in your mind and heart. For Temple, it was no different. I began, "Temple, I know you've had many painful moments in your life. During the movie, which scene brought you emotional pain?" There were a few moments of silence until Temple shared her memory with me. "The most painful parts were the teasing and bullying. There was one scene, at Scottsdale feed yard, with those cowboys leaning against the hay. It looked exactly like the real Scottsdale feed yard on that day I got thrown out of there, and that brought back a lot of memories." I could hear Temple getting upset at this point. She then continued, "It made me think of how I went straight to the Arizona Farmer Ranchman magazine office and got my press pass. That pass allowed me access into the big cattle conventions, and the Scottsdale Feed yard." I knew what a profound moment that was for her when she saw that scene, as we had already talked about the real event. I also realized that memorable day of her getting thrown out of the Scottsdale feed yard was a twist of fate. It spurred her on to go get that press pass, which opened some pretty big doors for Temple.

By now, you must be wondering what the proudest moment in that movie for Temple was. Here you go! "Temple, what made you most proud in that movie?" Without hesitation, Temple replied, "The proudest part of the movie was seeing all my projects! They did a scene in the movie where they showed off the optical illusion room. The real one that I showed off at school was the one with the trapezoidal window, and I was very proud of that. For the movie, I learned that the stage hands had a great deal of trouble with that."

I asked Temple about the original red squeeze machine. She stated, "When we moved, it got thrown out. Things have a way of getting into the trash when you're moving." I then wanted to know how she de-stresses herself these days, since she doesn't have a squeeze machine to use. Temple replied, "I do the virtual squeeze machine. I imagine it in my mind. I tend to get really tired and not as stressed these days."

I saw Temple's movie in 2012, about a year after it came out. At the time of its release, February 2010, I didn't yet know that I was on the autism spectrum. A few weeks ago I decided to watch the movie

Chapter 1

again, to see it now that I personally know Temple. I cried myself silly throughout most of the film. The next day Temple called, and I shared this event with her. She wanted to know why I cried so much. I stated, "Well, it's different now that I know you, and have listened to you tell me these actual events from your life. I felt your pain, your successes, and everything in between. I identify with so many things." I then said, "Of course, a movie can only be so long, and there's so much more about you that people will discover in this book."

"Yes, they will," Temple agreed.

CHAPTER 2
The Temple Machine

Have you ever wondered what it would be like to be world famous, recognized everywhere you go? I've gotten to know not only Temple, but those people closest to her that support everything she's doing. I know you are going to enjoy learning just what it takes to be a global phenomenon. Temple has a very demanding schedule and speaks all over the world, about both autism and animal handling. She also continues to work in the cattle industry. It takes several people to handle this grueling schedule. Teresa Corey, Temple's liaison, handles the autism side while Cheryl Miller, Temple's other liaison, tends to the animal side. During the eight months I worked on this book, I couldn't believe just how many places Temple was traveling to, multiple times per week, sometimes for weeks at a time. I decided to put this chapter early on to give you an idea of how demanding Temple's schedule really is. She just takes it all in stride and keeps on going.

I had the opportunity to interview Cheryl Miller, and here's what she shared with me.

"Cheryl, tell me how you first met Temple. Where was it?" I asked.

Cheryl replied, "I was hired in the Department of Animal Sciences as the administrative assistant to the department head, and I also did typing for a number of the professors. Temple was one of them. That's how I first met her, and that was about 1997. About ten years ago I was getting ready to retire, and I had mentioned that to Temple. She asked, 'Who's going to do my work for me?' and I said, 'Well, I can continue to work for you out of my home.' I live very close to her, only about a mile away. So, that's how that happened."

How well-known was Temple at the time you started working for her?" I inquired. Cheryl replied, "At that time, no one knew who Temple Grandin was, so I would only get a trickling of emails. Shortly after that, her movie came out, and things exploded! It was released February 6, 2010. I went to working six or seven days a week instead of just a few minutes a day. It got pretty serious. It's simply crazy, because she has so many speaking requests and she's been publishing a lot more as well." I gushed, "Wow! That's pretty amazing! That must have been quite an experience for you. Of course, for Temple as well, but you have to handle it all."

Cheryl continued, "Teresa deals with most of the autism speaking engagements, and Temple and I handle the rest. She also has an agent who gets speaking requests to Temple, and then we tend to that. Temple always makes her own flight reservations because she knows where she's going and where she's coming from. She's not always departing out of Denver, so she does everything regarding the flights. I'll handle Power Points, pictures, and getting in touch with the people who want her to come and speak."

I asked, "Do you ever go with her on any of these events?"

Chapter 2

"I do go with her to local events," Cheryl stated.

Cheryl also shared, "We go out to lunch quite often, and her friend and assistant Mark will go, too. Mark and I will joke and Temple doesn't laugh, and she says our humor is too sophisticated for her. She says such funny things. She gets a kick out of things that are kind of child-like, such as talking about vomiting. Silly, goofy things make her laugh, then she can't stop laughing. Anything about boogers, vomit, or anything that makes kids laugh will get her laughing her head off! She'll get bouts of uncontrolled laughter, which makes you start laughing, too. Temple has developed a really good sense of humor. She's also the most nonjudgmental person I've ever met, and very sensitive. She could get a thousand good reviews of her book on Amazon, but if she gets one bad one, she can dwell on it a long time. If somebody doesn't like something she said or wrote, it really bothers her."

"I'll share this with you, Cheryl, I'm just like that, too. So I totally understand that Temple gets like that."

Cheryl also tends to things regarding Temple's graduate students. "All of Temple's graduate students love her, and when they leave with their degree they all get excellent jobs and become very successful. One thing I'd really like for people to know is how Temple supports all her students. When they leave, they graduate with no debt. She pays their tuition and all expenses. Very few people know that. I'll get a bill from the accounting department of the school for a student for sixty, seventy, even eighty thousand dollars for their tuition, and Temple just writes out the check for that. That's why she does all those speaking engagements, because she uses the money she makes from them to pay for all her graduate students. That's pretty outstanding."

I stated, "When I heard Temple announce that at her birthday party, I nearly fainted. So, all these years she's been a silent philanthropist. That is so incredibly admirable. I truly feel proud to know her."

Cheryl went on to speak more on Temple's admirable qualities. She started, "I make her blank business cards, and the only thing on them is her picture. I make up about fifty to seventy-five at a time. She likes to put hand-written messages on them for kids. She goes through four to five hundred of these cards a year. I think that's pretty outstanding of her to do. She also takes calls from people who just want to ask her a question. Sometimes a kid will call saying they are going to write a report about her, and they'd like to interview her. She does call them back! Practically nobody at her level does that. Can you imagine being a little kid, and you're going to write a report about somebody famous, and they call you? How exciting for them. That will affect them the rest of their life, and they'll always remember that. Temple knows that." I smiled, stating, "Yes, there are many times she tells me she just got off the phone with a kid or young adult with autism that just called her. And she'll talk to them for an hour! It's unbelievable!"

"It's really an experience when you travel with her," Cheryl shared. "When we went to her induction into the Academy of Arts and Sciences, everybody just stared at her. Some people will come up to speak with her. Most people know who she is because they've seen the movie, and by the way she dresses. It's so interesting to watch, to be in the

Chapter 2

background seeing how people react to her. It's really cool, and lots of fun. At the Arts and Sciences event, there were all these world-famous scientists and artists, and Temple was the most sought-after one out of all of them! What's amazing is when we go to lunch in town, the same thing happens. We typically go to one of two restaurants. People will be looking at her, some will even come over to her to say something like 'thank you for all you've done,' or they'll say they saw her movie and really admire her. She's really humble about it, and she'll keep eating and talking after they're gone."

"Yes," I stated, "I know how humble she is. All her fame didn't change her. It didn't swell her head. That is very unique."

Cheryl told me this as well, "Temple also has no qualms about confronting people who are saying bad things, or wrong things about her. Once, up in Canada she was giving a talk about slaughter, and there was a group of protesters outside. She just walked right up to them and started talking to them. She's really gutsy like that! She's not afraid to go talk to them." I replied, "I would have liked to see their faces when Temple came walking towards them!"

CHAPTER 3
Down by the Seashore

Most everyone has childhood memories of family trips to the seashore, whether just for a day or weeks at a time. I can fondly remember the annual summer trip to Cape May, New Jersey for a week's visit. I figured Temple was no different than others, and I was correct. Think back to when you were a kid, did you go to the seashore? What do you recall?

"Temple," I prompted, "tell me about your times by the seashore when you were a kid." Temple replied, "Well, I used to love walking on the beach near where we lived in in Massachusetts, and collecting all kinds of sea shells. We went to Cape Cod in the summers. Then, when we'd get home, I loved to glue them onto a big piece of cardboard and make a mosaic. I made a big turtle, using the shells to make all the scales and small rocks to make the other parts of him. My aunt used to like to go out to the beach with us. She liked making those mosaics, so that's what we did. Kids these days aren't doing enough of those kinds of activities. I loved to walk on the beach, watch the waves coming in, and feel the sun on my shoulders. I'd sit down on the sand and spend hours just picking up the sand and letting it sift between my fingers. I loved that feeling. I also loved to fly kites on the beach. It was the best place to do that. This is what kids need to do! They need to learn to make things, like kites, and then go fly them."

I piped up, "It's like kids just don't play outside any more. They're inside on computers. But it's up to the parents to limit the time they spend doing that, and get them out doing old-fashioned kid stuff again."

"That's exactly right!" Temple added.

Temple's mind drifted back to those early days on the beach, "I loved making sand castles for hours and hours, with my little plastic bucket and tools. I really loved being on the beach. I enjoyed the smell of the salt air, and the sound of the wind blowing." I said, "I think those of us on the spectrum enjoy all these things more than others, because we see and feel every last detail that others miss. I loved doing all that, too, on the beach in Cape May."

Temple got excited sharing this with me, and her tone changed. "One of my happiest times on the beach was finding a bottle with a message in it. I was so excited! I ran all the way home with it, careful not to break it. It was an old chianti bottle, the basket long gone. I carefully opened the cork out of it, opened the message, and was a little disappointed because it only came from about two miles down the road. So, then I started putting messages into bottles and tossing them off boats, which was fun because I'd get people returning them to me." I was intrigued at Temple's story, and dug a little deeper. "When you wrote those messages and put them in the bottle, what did you write?" Temple replied, "I'd write, 'Dear Finder, this bottle was thrown off a boat (there was no GPS back then, so I'd describe where the boat was when

Chapter 3

I threw it in the water). I'd appreciate for you to write back when you find it, because I'd be interested to learn how far it's traveled.' I'd chuck them off the ferry when we were going to Martha's Vineyard, and I got letters back on about half of them. I always wrote the messages in pencil, so that even if the cork leaked and the note got water damage, the note was still legible."

"How often did you do that?" I inquired.

"I threw off about twenty bottles and got about ten of them back. The one that went the farthest went all the way up to Maine. They wrote back and said they were just looking for shells on the beach and happened to find the bottle with the message, and described where they found it. That was a really fun thing to do!"

There was one sensory issue that arose each time they went to Martha's Vineyard, which is typical for a person on the autism spectrum, child or adult. "Something I really hated was on the ferry to Martha's Vineyard—I hated the horn on that boat. Hated it. They'd blow the horn when they'd get into the harbor." "Well, how was that dealt with?" I asked. She replied, "So, there was a cabin below the deck. I can remember when I was a kid, flinging myself down on the deck and screaming because it hurt my ears. But then they started letting me ride below the deck, in the cabin. There were windows that I could look out through. You could still hear the horn, but it was much quieter down there in the cabin."

She continued, "I hated that ferry because of the horn, but I went on a ferry very similar to that last year and I stood right up on the deck under the wheel house. When they blew the horn I just flinched, that's all I did. I figured I had to conquer it."

CHAPTER 4
Christmas Memories

I loved hearing Temple's tales of her childhood Christmas memories. Being a visual thinker like her, I envisioned the scene she described in my mind, and it was very warm and cozy.

"Temple, tell me about Christmas time when you were a kid. What do you remember?" Temple perked up on this question, "I loved Christmas time! We had a ritual every Christmas Eve of decorating the Christmas tree, and I really liked that. We would cook steaks in the fireplace, and we knew it wasn't good for the fireplace, which is why we only did it once a year. But I really loved how the steak tasted from being cooked like that. That was a real treat!" I asked, "Did your family have an artificial tree, or a real one?" Temple replied, "We always got a real tree from somewhere in town where they would sell Christmas trees on the sidewalk, and there were special ornaments that we kept in a special box and used on it each year. There was one ornament that my mother absolutely hated. It was this hideous pink plastic angel that I'd put on the top of the tree. There were also these glass birds with bristle tails and clamps for feet that were very fragile, so we were extremely careful with those, and other special ornaments that mother kept from year to year. My sister and I would each put decorations on the tree, and learn to take turns doing things." Christmas is my favorite holiday, and I love to play carols throughout the season. "Temple," I asked, "were there Christmas carols playing while the tree was being decorated?" She reminisced, "Yes, most of the time we had them playing."

"What was your favorite Christmas present you ever received?" I asked. "One of my favorite Christmas presents was a Raleigh English-style bicycle," Temple told me. "I had graduated from the fat-tire kind to the English-style. I really liked that. Now the fat-tire bikes are back in style, but back in the fifties they were not very stylish. That was a really big deal. That was one of my favorite presents, it was the bike to have."

"I can imagine how thrilled you were with that bike, after working so hard to learn to ride it!" I stated.

"Temple, did you believe in Santa Claus?" I asked. "I did believe in Santa Claus, and then my sister went and spoiled it! She snuck downstairs and hid under the piano, and found out who Santa really was. I was about seven when that happened, so I was pretty young. Even before that, I used to wonder. I thought that even if reindeer could fly, there were still problems. How could he get down the chimney? I'd look at the fireplace and analyze that somebody couldn't fit through it. I was using my logical thinking about Santa Claus!"

"Oh, that's really funny. I can picture you trying to analyze all about Santa Claus," I laughed. I can remember the let-down when I discovered there wasn't a Santa Claus. How about you?

CHAPTER 5
Crazy Funny Stuff &
Childhood Memories

I'm dating myself, but I remember that fun kid's show *The Little Rascals*. I loved all the antics those kids got into! It was so much fun watching them. When Temple started sharing stuff that she did as a kid, it reminded me of that show, and I was laughing quite heartily. She was a prankster and fun-loving kid, and it seems like she just went non-stop. There was no sitting around for her! She did a lot of her activities with her sister, who is two years younger than her.

I suggest you make yourself a cup of coffee or tea, and plan to hang out here with me a while, as I've got lots to tell you. This chapter will take you back to your childhood days, and make you remember crazy, funny stuff you did, too. I hope you are sitting in your favorite cozy chair with your mug. I must first tell you that once Temple got on a roll telling me these things, she went one after another!

Temple started giggling before she even began to talk. "I can remember a really bad thing we did. A wet toilet paper fight over at a friend's house!" She went on, "In the living room, we had gobs of wet toilet paper and were slinging it onto the walls. This was at my next-door neighbor's house. When that kid's mother came home, it wasn't pretty!"

"Here's another thing we did," she went on, "we threw tomatoes over the garage and they landed in the next-door neighbor's car, which was a convertible—and they had the top down!" She punctuated this story with more fond laughs. "We didn't know that car was on the other side of the garage. We were using the tomatoes from the next-door neighbor's garden, all of them. That car was filled with tomatoes. Boy, was it a mess."

I stated, "Wow, Temple, I'm glad I wasn't your next-door neighbor!"

"The neighbor was extremely tolerant of our bad behavior," she said. "Oh, and we had mud fights in her garage, too!" That woman must have been a saint.

Leave it to Temple to add her own twist on things. She told me, "When I was a very young kid, I had a hockey table. Some of the neighbor's kids and I liked to put like a hundred marbles on it, and just keep hitting all the marbles into the goal. That was a lot more fun than just using the hockey puck! That was one of my favorite games. And the thing is, you've got to do that with other people."

Are you starting to see just how much Temple was getting out there and simply doing things? She wasn't sitting around focused on the fact that she had autism—far from it.

Playing Terminal Chess

Temple's next-door neighbor's house seemed to be a fun place to get into some mischief. Temple once glued a bedroom door shut! She shared, "Fortunately, the kid's mom came home before the door got glued shut permanently. It wasn't super glue, as that didn't exist then. It was epoxy."

Temple's mind was never idle, she was always coming up with something new and creative to do. Temple told me about a chess set that she used the soldering iron on. "That was when we were in elementary school. We played what we called 'terminal chess.' When a chess piece would get taken off the board, we'd 'kill it with the ray gun.' That meant melting it onto the ping-pong table with a soldering iron!"

I'm surprised the next-door neighbors didn't ban Temple from coming over there—I'd suspect they actually got some amusement out of her antics.

Staging Fake Baths

"It sounds like you and your sister played a lot together," I said. "I'm guessing you were always the ringleader." Temple replied, "One thing my sister and I spent a lot of time doing was staging fake baths! We went through this big elaborate process to pretend that we took a bath, to fool our mother. I was about ten, and my sister was about eight. So, we'd carefully fill the tub up, splash around the water and make a whole lot of noise, then we'd make wet foot prints all over the floor and wet the towels. We'd spend a whole lot of time and effort staging these fake baths. (Temple was now giggling uncontrollably.) I'd crinkle up the towels just right, totally wet the washcloths ... we'd spend more time staging the bath than if we had simply just taken one. Of course, that was my idea." I was shaking my head and rolling my eyes at this point.

I will tell you that I wasn't such a creatively naughty kid like Temple was. Do you see what I mean? She's talking about being a young kid, but was doing things that involved actual planning to carry out. Just wait—it gets better.

"Temple," I asked, "were there ever any dances at your school, any social events?" Her reply was, "Oh yes, there were dances. I never got picked to dance. Only if it was ladies' choice, then I'd pick someone to dance." "So," I replied, "what was your motivating factor, what made you pick a certain guy?" She responded, giggling, "I'd pick the one that had been avoiding me."

I thought that was a grand answer—very savvy!

Front Lawn Camping and Drink Stand

You can guess that Temple was the commanding officer for this venture! "Another fun thing we did was have a sleepout on the front lawn. We used an old army tent from a friend's garage that we didn't even know how to put together. We never got any help from an adult, never! We'd pitch the tent that was missing half the pieces, so it sagged. Do you think the adults helped us at all? We had to figure it out on our own. I can remember freezing because my sleeping bag wasn't heavy enough for that weather. We'd have meetings to plan for all the candy, grape soda, and chips we were going to get! We would all use our allowances, so we learned how to manage money. We were around ten years old; my sister was a little younger, around eight."

Chapter 5

Temple's early days as an entrepreneur had to start somewhere! "Then, there was my disastrous drink mix stand. That's when I learned how much sugar was in these drink mixes. I took a bookcase outside and put a little sign on it, stating it that I was going to have a drink stand. The first pitcher went well, I earned a dollar and change. The next pitcher tasted horrible, because I only had half the amount of sugar. That's when I learned you need to have all necessary supplies. Well, that's the basic thing in business, you need to have enough supplies."

Oh sure, that's what every little kid is thinking.

Superman!

Temple has a very silly side that you'll see here. "Once, I went over a neighbor kid's house, and there were these sticks about three feet long in his yard. He told me they were kryptonite, and if I touched the ends of the sticks, I'd die. I didn't really believe that, but I didn't dare touch the ends of the sticks, just in case. It shouldn't have mattered, though, because I wasn't Superman! Oh, yeah, Superman was my favorite comic book hero—I was a huge Superman fan. I had the first Superman annual. When we moved, it got thrown out. I bet that thing would be worth a lot today."

"I never read my comic books under the covers (like in movies), but I would tell myself stories under the covers then laugh my head off over them." I inquired, "Temple, what kind of stories would you tell yourself?" She replied, "There were these shows: *The Little Rascals:*

Our Gang. I thought those shows were a real riot, so I would tell myself stories about pranks they'd do at my school and things like that."

Fun With Costumes

Wait until you hear this zany thing Temple did! "Once there was a dog show at school, but my mother didn't want our dog to spend the day at school. So, I made up a costume of a dog, and I went to school dressed as a dog, and I had other students 'show' me. We had a golden retriever back then, his name was Lannie. So my dog costume was white pants, a white tee shirt, and I made the dog head mask out of a bed sheet that I colored up with crayons."

I said to Temple, "You sure were into costumes back then!" She replied, "Yes! I'd go watch my mother perform in shows, like the time she was dressed as a mermaid. She had on a bright green shimmering mermaid tail. During that play, my sister and I got to go up on stage and pick numbers out of a hat for the door prizes. We had a costume box at home that had all kinds of old clothes in it, and somewhere along the way I got a derby hat and some 1930s bathing suits. We'd dress up in those as clown suits."

Temple was on a roll with all this. "We put a lot of plays on when I was a kid. It would be my sister, maybe one or two kids from next door, and me. We'd make costumes, of course. I made a lot of costumes. I made some really elaborate ones when I was in high school. My roommate and I wanted to be Mr. Ed one year for the school's Halloween party, so we used surplus grey army flannel to make the costume; we

Chapter 5

even made a stall in the corner of the room. I had to be the rear end, because my roommate said she would only do it if she could be the head. Another time I was an astronaut, with an elaborate helmet that lit up. I wore that to a horse show that had a costume class. I had to work really hard to make the horse, King, tolerate the spacesuit!"

This one is a gem. Temple shared, "Another elaborate costume was pretty funny. The school I attended was on a lot of land, and there was a graveyard on it with the original owner's grave there. That graveyard was right next to the outdoor riding arena. There was big monument there of Jones Warren Wilder. So, I went as Wilder dead in the coffin, and my friend went as the monument. I'd found this pink fluorescent smoking jacket and wore that, as I thought he probably died like that, and I put white powder all over my face to look like a skull."

This was one of my favorites. She told me, "There was a mountain lion that had been spotted a few times near the parking lot that we named George, so the following Halloween I dressed as George. I spent a lot of time making costumes while I was in high school, not a lot of time studying. I spent a lot of time cleaning horse stalls, too. The one thing I was doing was learning how to work, something not too many people are doing now."

Smiling, I said, "I can count on you to always be thinking logically!"

Fun at the Elementary School Fair

Temple sure has a theatrical side. She told me, "My elementary school used to have a fair every year, a really nice fair. Mother would always put on a play during the fair. One year, they put on *The Wizard of Oz*. I can remember that one of the parents played the witch, and there was a huge green box where the Wizard was. Mother got some pyrotechnics to set off from somewhere she worked, and that was pretty impressive. Another time the play was *Ferdinand the Bull*, and I remember our next-door neighbors found plastic horns to put on their head for cattle horns. It was a very creative, fun thing that was done with all the kids!"

"There were other fun things, too, like play makeup. We would put on all this makeup and get our picture taken with an instant camera, which was a new thing back then!"

Temple went on, "We actually had a .22 rifle shooting range at our little fair. All the dads were in on that. They were very careful with us, and we got to shoot the .22's into the side of a hill with targets. They had a mechanism that would pull the targets in and out, so no one had to go near the target area. After the fair was over, I'd go down with the boys to the target area and dig the bullets out of the wood."

Party Crashing and Neighborly Feuds

Get a load of this; crashing a party takes on a whole new meaning. Temple starts giggling again as she tells me, "One of the funniest things I did was at one of my mother's parties. I got a hanger and put a dress on it, got a paper bag and made it look like a head, and drew a face on it to put on the hanger. My room was right over the screened-in porch where everyone at the party was. I dropped the hanger down on a string and quickly pulled it right back up. Everyone screamed! I only did that once—only once!"

I think I'd be afraid to go over Temple's place! Laughing to herself even more, Temple shared, "I loved to do other mischievous things, like rig up a box over a door filled with confetti. When someone came to the door, it would turn upside down and dump all the confetti all over them. These are the kinds of things I did, I was twelve and under. I was creatively naughty!" How did Temple dream these things up?

"Another great memory I have of our neighborhood was rooting for the Harvard and Yale football games. My dad went to Harvard, so we were Harvard fans. Our next-door neighbors were Yale fans. One time, they decorated the entire neighborhood in bright blue crepe paper, but it rained, and all the blue dye went all over the neighborhood's front porches and fences! Thankfully, I didn't do that—but I did learn from it. One time we decorated for Harvard, and used pink toilet paper because we knew it wouldn't stain. I used that pink toilet paper to decorate the neighbor's house, too. Then I made up a bumper sticker, went into the neighbor's house, and stuck it on the front of their car so they wouldn't see it when they came into the garage. They drove to church with the bumper sticker that said, 'We're Harvard Fans!' Those neighbors pulled pranks on us, too, of course. At election time, they came over and put all kinds of Nixon stickers all over our car, inside and out."

Horse Activities

Can you picture this in your mind? "When I was in elementary school, around third or fourth grade, we'd play horse. Because I was big and strong, I'd be the horse and the other kids got to ride me! I never got to ride them because they weren't big enough. At our house we had a green rug, so that was the pasture, the other house had a brown rug, so that was the corral. We made bits out of pencils, and used string for the reins. Then you'd put the pencil in your mouth, with the string coming from both sides."

Let's fast-forward a little to high school, where Temple thought of good times with her roommate. "When I was in high school, my roommate and I had plastic horses. We didn't play with them, we decorated them! I made bridles for them, and fancy western parade outfits. I'd use black shoelaces to make the bridle and breastplate. Then, I'd get silver foil from a cigarette box to make the tiny silver trimmings. We'd spend endless hours making beautiful western parade outfits for them, and then display them. Then, the grandkids of the headmaster got to play with them, and it was a great honor for those grandkids to come and play with our horses. When I graduated, I gave the horses to those kids. One of the horses got a broken leg, so I made a prosthetic leg for it and carefully painted it to match the rest of the horse. We made Arabian outfits, parade outfits, and just had a great time doing that together!" Temple was developing her skills at interpersonal relations way back then.

Chapter 5

The Flying Saucer Hoax

Temple went on to recall more antics. "I can remember the crazy flying saucer hoax I pulled off when I was in high school. I had my whole school believing it. I made a classic fifties-style flying saucer, about eighteen inches across and round, out of two pieces of cardboard. It had a dome on top that I used a clear Dairy Queen bowl to make, and I put a light in it so the dome lit up. I then went up on the roof of the far end of the girls' building. Just as soon as they turned out their lights, I swung it back and forth in front of their window. The first time they didn't see it, but I swung it past their window again, and that time they screamed! Then I ran back down to my room, and then I heard them all talking about the flying saucer they just saw, to which I kept saying, 'That's nonsense, that's nonsense.' The weird thing was that a couple weeks later there was a UFO sighting that was written up in the newspaper! The girls were convinced that what they saw out their window that night was the same UFO. It wasn't until a few years later at graduation that I went up to the two girls that saw my flying saucer and handed it to them, stating, 'This is what you saw out your window two years ago that night.'"

Laughing, I said, "Oh, I'm sure they were pretty shocked!"

"Here's another one from high school," Temple recalled. "There were a bunch of girls that liked stealing my candy. So, I got those little licorice logs that were wrapped, unwrapped them, filled them with shampoo, and rewrapped them." Temple was now giggling rather un-controllably. "Yeah, these girls would come in my room and take stuff.

Once I took my sandwich cookies, took them apart, and replaced the white cream filling with toothpaste! Nothing dangerous, just make it so the cookies wouldn't taste too good. Eventually, those kids stopped taking stuff from me."

I'm just picturing those girls biting into all that stuff!

"As an adult, I'll still do funny things," she told me. "When I was on a plane, I watched some gross movie about a giant snake in a big fancy ballroom, and I'd start laughing so hard and loud that people were turning around looking at me." I'm sure those sitting nearby weren't very pleased at that! "I think the silliest things, like that, are really funny. My taste in movies ranges from action, to science fiction, to really serious."

Favorite Movies

Before continuing with Temple's antics, I'd like to take this opportunity to share with you her favorite movies. It's quite fascinating.

I asked Temple, "Which other movies do you like?" Temple had just returned home, where she watched a movie along the way. "Well, I just watched the third *Planet of the Apes* on a plane. I like the one where the ape was in the research lab, where the apes became partly human and were living in the woods, and the airline pilot with a bloody nose spread the virus all around the world that's going to wipe out a lot of people. I actually like that one better than the one I saw on the plane today. Oh! There was another movie I just loved: *The Martian*. I read the book first, and I really enjoyed them both."

Chapter 5

"Another movie I thought was fantastic was *Hidden Figures*. That was just fantastic! It was about the women that did all the hand-calculations for the orbits of the Mercury and Gemini programs, and John Glenn's first orbital flight. It was all hand-calculated, and they were really discriminated against. One of the things I liked about Katherine Johnson, the woman portrayed in *Hidden Figures*, is that math came first. It was all about math. I can really relate to the scene where they weren't going to let a woman into the planning project meeting. That was a great movie."

Temple continued, "The thing is, I've always been a NASA fan, but back in the sixties and seventies no one knew they existed. They were doing all those calculations, and I never knew about it until the movie came out. When I recently got inducted into the Women's Hall of Fame, the press asked me who I would recommend, and I said Katherine Johnson. She was the head of the *Hidden Figures* women. She deserved to be in the Women's Hall of Fame. They never got any credit for any of that. Finally, Obama gave them the recognition they deserved. But for all those years, the Mercury and Gemini sub-orbital flights were done with hand-calculations. Then, when John Glenn went into space, these women had to figure out how to program the IBM 360 with punch cards. However, John Glenn didn't trust the IBM 360, so he wanted Katherine Johnson and the others to re-do the calculations. On the first orbital flight, the calculations are very critical. You have this capsule going around the earth, and if you re-enter too steeply, you burn up. If you re-enter too shallowly, you'd skip off the outer surface of the atmosphere and bounce into outer space. So, the angle had to be calculated perfectly. I really liked that movie, it was better than the book."

"Wow," I said, "I've got to get this movie. I never knew any of this, either, until now."

Temple has more favorites. "I really loved *Avatar* ... of course, way back when, there were movies like *2001: A Space Odyssey*. I loved *2001: A Space Odyssey*." I asked her if she liked *Apollo 13*. "Yes!" she responded excitedly, "In fact, I learned when I went to Cape Kennedy that *Apollo 13* is actually used in training because it's done so well. They had to figure out how to deal with emergencies. Those movies I really loved!"

Now that you know, we shall return to the crazy, funny stories!

We Ship Anything, Anywhere!

Here comes Temple's zany side again! I knew it was going to be a piece of work by the way she started giggling. "Here's something really funny," she began. "I laughed so hard about this that I got a coughing fit. Brad Masella (who works for Future Horizons) and I were once driving along on a highway, and there was a truck in front of us that said, 'We ship anything, anywhere!' I said, 'Do you want to bet? I'll give you a load you'll never ship, ever! I'd make up a box inside a box, big enough to fit on a pallet, and I'd fill it with pig guts packed in a frozen ice box! I'd load it so it would look normal. But then as they'd get half way across the country, it would be hot—I could just see them at some weigh station!'" She laughed to herself. "By then the ice would have melted, with the liquid dripping out of the box and out of their trailer! The smell would be horrible, and then they'd open the box and the pig guts would spill out all over! We have a weigh station here in Fort Collins. I was just picturing the liquid dripping out of the truck!" Temple was laughing so hard at this vision she had created in her mind. I had it envisioned in my mind, too, and I got a bit queasy.

Experience in the Hospital

I wish I were a fly on the wall for this. Temple told me, "In the early nineties, I had to have surgery. I can remember walking down to the nurses' station and talking with them about all kinds of weird things, it was a lot of fun. I was telling them stories about slaughter houses, and they told me this story about this one prisoner who came there all the time. He had a colostomy, and he'd put ketchup in the colostomy bag, so it looked like he was bleeding, and get trips to the hospital!"

"I did okay as a patient, I woke up right away after surgery. The other patient in my room puked all night, and she had these plastic things on her legs that inflated, so I heard 'pssssttt' (an imitation of the noise) on-and-off all night. I had to keep pressing the nurses call button each time the patient next to me started vomiting again. Then they woke me up at six in the morning to take a blood test. I said, 'You've got to be kidding! I didn't get any sleep.' Luckily, I have a pretty high tolerance for pain; I only took some pain medication for the first day, then I was just careful not to stand too long. I got three book chapters written in that time."

"Then, a week after my surgery, I went over to the meat plant. We were just supposed to meet in the shop. Once there, the guys wanted to go out into the plant, and they started climbing over gates! I said, 'Wait a minute, I just had major surgery! I can't climb over a gate!' Ten days after my surgery, I made a trip to Cincinnati. I took the tiniest bag I had, just over my shoulder, so I didn't have to lift anything heavy. I had a big incision. I also remember once when I had surgery back in the seventies, by the time I woke up from the surgery I had missed dinner, and I was really mad. Finally, the nurses brought me some of their private stash. I told them I was going to order a pizza!"

Whew! Temple must be filled with batteries; she just keeps on going!

Shingle-Throwing Contests

I call this one "dangerous kid stuff." Have you ever done this? I can't say I have. This was when Temple was in boarding school. "Some of the most fun adventures we had were in the summer. I can remember roofing the horse barn at school. I thought that was a lot of fun, shingling the roof. We had no fall protection. Things were different back in the sixties. There were other students who were doing it, too. They were all boys. We had a lot of fun throwing shingles! We'd cut off edges to make them fit, then get the leftover pieces and throw them like frisbees while we were on the roof. One day while we were up on the roof, there was a partial eclipse. That was a real experience! We all knew it was coming. Not much work got done during that time. It was interesting to see how it got partially darkened. Everyone told us not to look at it, but we did quick glances just to see it."

Regarding nature, she went on, "When I was in Hawaii about fifteen years ago, I got to see a volcano erupt! I watched the lava flow down all the way to the road, where it just stopped. The lava was about eighteen inches thick. It was very impressive to see that, and to walk on it. The road just disappeared under the lava."

Temple is a weather buff, just like me. She said, "I love to watch storms; I like to watch The Weather Channel, and see all kinds of storms. Sometimes I can't believe those crazy people who chase them." I replied, "Me, too! Have you ever seen the show where you ride in the cockpit of the hurricane hunter plane and fly through the eyewall?" She replied, "Yes! I love watching that, too!"

Endless Science Questions to Engineering Grandfather

"When I was a child, we had a great telescope at my grandfather's house. You could see down to the harbor, and see people on boats having parties. You could see them drinking, doing everything! I did that a lot. Indeed, I was a mischievous child!" I'm wondering: just what was she watching?

Temple's voice changed a bit when she mentioned her grandfather, who was an engineer. I asked her, "It sounds like you enjoyed being with your grandfather. Were there any other fun memories you have of him?" When she responded, I could tell those were some very happy memories for her. It made me smile just picturing a young

Temple sitting there with her inquisitive mind, presenting him with one question after another. Even as a child, her thirst for knowledge was unquenchable.

"Oh yes, Sundays with Grandfather. We'd go into the study, and he'd be smoking his pipe, and all his Scientific American journals were in there. All the rest of the family would be in the living room, except for Grandfather and me. I'd just be asking him one question after another. You know, why is the sky blue, why is the grass green? Why do the tides come in and out? We'd go to the beach a lot, so I'd see the tides go in and out. He'd explain it in great detail, how the moon goes around and pulls on the water . . . the gravitational pull on the water which controls the tide."

She went on, remembering more details. "Oh, yes! There were the locks and channel, and the tide gates. We'd go to our summer house that was on a harbor, and it was all closed in except for where there was a bridge with tide gates in it. When the tide would start to go out, the doors would close and keep the water in the small lagoon so it wouldn't be all nasty mud, and just stay nice all the time. They kind of looked like locks in a canal. When the tide came in the gates would open, then when it went out they'd shut. They were set up in the shape of a "V", big heavy wooden things. Grandfather and I would walk out there and look at them, trying to be there when the tide turned, and he'd explain how they worked."

"This was my grandfather from Mother's side. He's the one who co-invented the autopilot. We'd stand on the bridge, see, and the tide gates were underneath the bridge." I interrupted Temple for a moment: "I can see where you got your scientific mind from!" Continuing, Temple said, "Yes! Grandfather and I would be in that study talking about science, while everyone else was in the living room. We visited maybe five times a year, but when we did go, it was on a Sunday. I was in elementary school at that time, in third or fourth grade. I remember looking at a power plant belching out black smoke. I wasn't with grandfather then, we were having a family picnic. I said to my mother, won't that make the atmosphere dirty? I might have been around eight or nine, I was little. I watched that black smoke going into the sky, and I had learned in class about the atmosphere. If you take the Earth as an apple, the atmosphere is only as thick as the skin. So, I got to thinking that the black smoke would dirty up the atmosphere. Mother then said that it just goes into the sky and disappears. So, it turns out I was right."

Always Being Observant

I stated, "You are always very observant of everything going on around you, things that others don't notice."

Temple shared with me the day of the solar eclipse, where she was walking along at Colorado State University. It was time for the eclipse to occur. As she walked along, she was looking down on the sidewalk. Suddenly, she saw hundreds of shadows on the sidewalk of the eclipse, which she realized were coming from between the leaves on the tree. The tree leaves were acting like multiple pin-hole cameras. She stopped to take photos of it, as others simply walked right on by and didn't see it all. She went on, "And of course, the eclipse shadows on the sidewalk at Colorado State University, no one else noticed. I've been showing the slide of that, just the other day to an audience of six hundred people, and only about ten knew what the shadows were on the sidewalk. Then I looked it up online, and found there's all kinds of eclipse shadows from the image coming between the leaves."

Special, Good Times at Family Gatherings

Continuing on the subject of her grandparents, she went on to talk about Sunday dinners at Granny's house. I know you are loving these stories as much as I am.

Temple recalled these special moments. "I'll tell you about Sunday dinner at Granny's house, where you had to display good manners and were only allowed to tell a story twice. That's right, manners were very important, and mother would tell me when it was someone else's turn to talk. It was the same at aunt Bella's, who was my father's sister. She had a big long hallway in her house, and she had a mirror at the end of the hall. So, after lunch, I'd run down the hall and watch as I'd get bigger in the mirror the closer I got to it. Then when we went to Granny's, she lived on the fifth floor, so I'd play 'beat the elevator.' I could run up five flights of stairs faster than the elevator could get up there! I was allowed to race the elevator when we came in and when we went out, but I wasn't allowed to do it all day because banging up and down the stairs would bother too many people. That was a way I could blow off steam, all that running. I really loved running down

Chapter 5

that hall and watching myself get bigger in the mirror. And I always beat the elevator." I'm thinking that Temple could have made it to the Olympics for running.

She kept on going, "There were special toys kept at Granny's house—they had a little wind-up bear that would walk, move his head, then start walking again. There was a squirrel that would hop when you wound it up, and a fishing set with magnets you'd use to catch the fish." "Oh, wow! I used to play that game with the fish, too!" I chirped in. Temple continued, "Those were the special toys that we just had at Granny's. So, when the grown-ups just wanted to sit around and talk, we'd go into the guest room and play with those toys. I really liked the fish with the magnets game."

I wanted you to hear about all of Temple's fun childhood antics. She was always active and interacting with others. Everything she did back then was setting the foundation for her future. She was learning life skills. This is very important for development, especially for children on the autism spectrum. Like Temple keeps saying, "Just get out there and do stuff!"

CHAPTER 6
Thrilling Events in Temple's Life!

The whole world will be excited to hear this one: I asked Temple for the most exciting, thrilling moment of her life. She thought for a few moments, then said, "Well, I might need a few minutes to answer that one. I can remember once galloping full speed on a horse, we were going really fast, and it was exhilarating. We were out in the woods on a dirt road. It was a really good feeling, a very thrilling experience. It was a beautiful summer day. I was riding Bat Lady, my favorite horse, with my forward seat English saddle. She was the one I rode in the shows; we just called her Lady for short. She was a beautiful bay, but I never knew what breed she was. I remember it like a little movie clip, it was a dirt road where we knew there would be no obstacles. It was flat out, all out galloping for about two minutes."

What was the most thrilling thing you've ever done?

Temple was still thinking about her horse days. "Another time we were galloping along on a dirt road, and there was a mud puddle, and I ended up flying over the horse's head and into the mud puddle! That wasn't any good." I shared, "I've been there and done that, too. I think anyone who's been riding horses has experienced a lovely moment like this."

She went on, "I remember the time Mr. McCallister—our riding instructor, who was a really heavy smoker—had dropped cigarette ash down into the hole on the front of the western saddle. There was smoke coming out of the front of the saddle, and I said, 'Mr. McCallister, your horse is on fire!' He jumped off the horse and pulled the saddle off, and the ash had burned a two-inch hole in the pad! Fortunately, it didn't burn the horse."

What a surprise, Temple the "creatively naughty" kid strikes again! "At the boarding school, we were only supposed to ride with a faculty member. Of course, I did something kind of naughty. I'd sneak out and go riding down in the pasture when nobody was around. It wasn't Lady, it was usually one of the easier horses when I did that. I'd ride bareback, and use this little thing I'd made out of parachute cord as a halter that I kept in my pocket. It was like a hackamore, with reins. I used that same thing to put on the horses when the farrier would come. When I snuck in those rides, yes, I'd enjoy the scenery, the movement of the horse, but most of all I'd get satisfaction out of being naughty and sneaking the ride!" I'll tell you, the galloping horse story kind of surprised me. As someone who's been riding since about twelve, I never did that. I'd have been too scared to go all-out galloping. Temple was kind of a dare-devil kid!

Making Things Work

Temple is all about her projects, and she really gets excitement out of making them work. "Another thing that gave me a thrill was making the dip vat work," she told me. "Just like they show in the movie, I got really excited over that! Having my design actually work made me very happy. You know, equipment start-ups are stressful; you are starting a new system, like when we started up the center track restrainers, and you wonder if things are going to work. Your responsibility is making things work." Temple takes that word, "responsibility," very seriously. There's no exception to that. She puts her heart and soul into everything she does. Continuing, Temple said, "When things don't work, you have to sort of figure it out at the spur of the moment, because you have to fix it. I can remember when we made the center track restrainer for adult cattle. The cattle wouldn't relax. I used a piece of cardboard to block their vision, and they settled down. It's extremely stressful when you are actually inventing new equipment and you have to make it work. The plant manager expects that it's going to work perfectly when you first start it up, so he's throwing a fit when it doesn't function perfectly in the first fifteen minutes. Yet I'm happy because it is working, and I know we can get it up to full production. When you're inventing something new, it doesn't always work perfectly, and you have to figure it out as you go." Temple went on, "Another interesting thing is going to meat packing plants, looking at all the antiquated equipment there, and figuring out how to build things that work. I really get a thrill out of designing stuff, then figuring out how to make it run!"

I love this one, and you will too! Temple got all gushy when she said, "Another exciting moment was at the Emmys! That was extremely exciting, wondering who's going to win; it's a total secret. I jumped up and then the boom camera came over to me! I was so excited. I tried to keep it in perspective: that it was exhilarating, but that's not real life. After that, I had to go to a cattle meeting, and there I was on a flight at six in the morning. In the middle seat on the plane I said, 'Welcome back to the real world!'"

"In his book, *An Astronaut's Guide to Life on Earth*, astronaut Mark Hadfield wrote about how he dealt with having gone to the International Space Station and doing a spacewalk, then returning back to Earth to build a deck on the back of the house. He wrote, 'I get satisfaction in the little things.' It's kind of a let-down, but you have to keep it in perspective. Those peak moments in your life are not going to be your real life. But being at the Emmys was a really thrilling moment, anyway! I hugged Emily Gersin Saines really tightly, then I hollered out to Mother, 'I know you're really nervous, stand up!' I had on a black cowboy shirt with studs that my sister gave me, and it's actually a Ralph 'La-Rain', Ralph 'La-REN' shirt!" You would love to hear Temple say it, because it's just grand the way she pronounced it.

CHAPTER 7
Getting Bullied & Teased in High School

Many people are bullied in high school, but it is even more common for those on the autism spectrum. It can be one of the most challenging times of a person's life. Temple had many great times in high school, and many bad times as well. Read on.

Temple talked about the point in her life that went from happy to not-so-happy: her high school days. "A big high school wasn't for me. I was happy up to that point, but that's when the bullying started. When I was in ninth grade, my reading and writing were at an adult level, and I could do all my elementary school math, but algebra was a problem. I got thrown out of a school." Pausing, I inquired, "Why did you get thrown out of school?" Temple replied, "For throwing a book at a girl—she called me a retard, so I threw a book at her." I certainly understood why Temple resorted to throwing a book at that girl. Rightly so! I personally think they should have thrown out that girl, not Temple.

Temple went on to say this, "When I was a young kid, I was all about projects. I loved to do projects. I got along with other kids because they like doing projects, too, so there was a common interest. Then, when I got into puberty and there were different kinds of emotions, that's when trouble started for me, because the other kids weren't interested in making projects anymore. They became interested in other things like clothes, jewelry—things I had no interest in. That's when all the bullying started. Up until then I never got bullied. When I was in elementary school the teacher explained to the other kids that I had a disability, something that you couldn't see, like a wheelchair. So, life was good up until puberty, when I turned fourteen."

Temple continued, "I then went away to Hampshire County School in Ridge, New Hampshire. I spent the next three years doing horse barn management, carpentry, costume making, and things I liked. I didn't do any studying until Mr. Carlock came along in my last year. But during those three years I was learning how to work, which is one of the most important things you can learn. I still had to be on time, and attend classes and the dining hall. I was not allowed to become a recluse in my room, absolutely not! Mr. Henry Patey, the headmaster, kept track of me. I had a good roommate there, too. We rode horses together, and talked about horses all the time. We'd do things like decorate those plastic horses and make costumes for them."

I asked Temple, "How did you feel about going away to boarding school?" She replied, "When I first went away to boarding school, it wasn't easy. It was pretty difficult for me in the beginning. Eventually, I got into riding and other things. The day Mother drove me there I was alright about it." I wondered, "Well, how did you feel as you watched her drive away?" She went on, "Yes, it was difficult getting dropped off there. Like in the movie, I cried a lot, and got into some fights. The school took horseback riding away, but I still had to clean out the stalls."

At first, Temple didn't want to do social activities at the boarding school, like attend movie night. So, here's what happened next. "Temple," I said, "I heard that you didn't want to attend movie night. How did that go?" Temple answered, "Well, they made me be the projectionist; I ran the movie projector. That way I could walk around during the movie. I almost got electrocuted by that projector, because I touched the light switch and the projector at the same time. I was turning the lights off as I turned on the projector, and I got fried across one hand to the other. It was one of those old sixteen-millimeter movie projectors. So, I did get to watch the movie, too, only standing. The reason they put me to work as the projectionist was that they weren't going to allow me to stay holed up in my room. I had to participate in everything with the other students. It was Mr. Patey who made me do it all. Even though I didn't study for the first three years, I had to attend the classes, I had to attend the meals, I had to attend chapel, and I was not allowed to be disruptive."

"There were definitely some people I was friends with. There were also some bullies—mostly the boys. Pretty much all people on the spectrum were bullied. Steve Jobs was bullied at school, Elon Musk was bullied at school, and then there's Wozniak. He got bullied." It doesn't take much for cause to be a victim of bullying at school. But when you are different, you have waving red flags over your head that say, "bully me!" Myself, and everyone I know and have read about who is different, were bullied in school.

This made Temple very sad. "One of the things that the other students called me was tape-recorder. I didn't understand why. But it was because I was always using the same phrases. The only place I wasn't bullied was where there was a shared interest, like electronics, model rockets, or horses. I can't emphasize enough the importance of getting these kids (with autism) involved with those of shared interests."

Hormones certainly do put a different spin on things. Temple experienced this in her own way. "I went to a large, all-girls high school. Once puberty hit, that's when everything changed for me. I was really happy up to that point. But then the girls were no longer interested in projects. They were interested in clothes, fashion, and boys. I had no interest in any of that." This is typical for females on the autism spectrum. Another problem Temple suffered at puberty was horrendous panic attacks. She discusses how she handled panic attacks in her book, *Thinking in Pictures*, which I highly recommend.

Temple continued, "There were no such things as video games back then when I was a kid, and mother restricted the amount of television that we could watch to one hour on weeknights and two hours on the weekend. That was highly restricted. You don't ban it, I never recommend banning it, but put limits on it." To all the parents of kids on the spectrum, listen up to this one. You have the power to regulate your child's time on that machine. Temple and I talk all the time about the kids "addicted" to video games; it should never have gotten to that point. And if it has, then it's time to make changes. Like Temple said, you don't just stop it, but put limits on it. Then adhere to them. I also suggest that you only have the computer in an area where you can see what your child is looking at, like in the kitchen, or anywhere nearby where the parent can monitor the kid. Leaving a child on a computer in their room with the door shut is only an invitation for bad choices to be made.

Temple liked to talk about early learning of life lessons, "When I was seven and eight, I learned a lot. I learned how to save money. I got fifty cents a week for my allowance, and if I wanted a kite and some string, I'd have to save for two weeks. That was an important lesson to learn."

The Importance of Mentors

I asked Temple who her role models were when she was young. "Well, Mother, of course. Then there were other people, Mr. Carlock, and Ann . . . but I'd rather call them mentors. There was also a good contractor who sought me out to do design work for him, Jim Uhl. And then there were the people out there who did the bad stuff to me, like the ones who put bull testicles on my vehicle, who you saw in the movie. They were the foremen, not the feed lot owners, but the cowboy foremen. They were the same ones who put the metal plate in the dip vat and messed it all up. You know, they didn't like this nerd girl coming in on their turf." In the long run, both the good and the bad can all be teachable moments.

Temple is always logical. "Talking about teachable moments, when I was a kid, manners were a very important thing to be taught. I can remember when I was in second or third grade, the school cafeteria served chocolate ice cream and I licked it like a dog. They picked up my dessert and said, 'You are not a dog.' That was all they said. So, I had no dessert that day. Did I throw a fit about that? No, I didn't. That's how kids were taught manners back then. I think it's really bad to not have structured manners these days."

Temple feels strongly about bringing back classes at high school that do hands-on projects. "One of the things I really enjoyed at school was jewelry-making class. I had lots of fun making things. We also had class for making costumes! I really enjoyed that, too!"

Physical activity is a great thing for kids on the autism spectrum. "We had volleyball, and I really liked that. I was pretty decent at that, and even won an award for it."

"Temple, you sure were into a lot of physical activity back then," I stated. She replied, "I was really active when I was young. Now I just do my back strengthening exercises each night for my sciatic nerve, which are stretches and sit-ups. I do one hundred sit-ups every night because they help me sleep. And I hate every one of them!"

I guess they help me sleep too, as I get tired just thinking of it!

CHAPTER 8
Crazy About Horses!

Everyone saw in the movie *Temple Grandin* that she was involved with horses while in high school. She first rode horses in her younger days, but it was at the high school boarding school where horses became a big part of her life.

"So, Temple, what were your favorite things about horses?" I asked. "I really liked riding them, and getting ready for shows," she told me. "We'd go to little shows, and there was a lot of preparation getting the horse ready for them. I'd go in the equitation classes, where you're judged how well you ride, so I'd practice that. I also jumped horses over small jumps, only like two-foot-high fences. I had to have just the right saddle, one with forward padded knee rolls, as that kept me from falling off."

As you've already seen, Temple liked to put on a show! "Tell me about the glitz and glamour side of things," I piped up. She quickly replied, "Banners and flags! In the Cowgirl Hall of Fame Museum in Fort Worth, Texas is one of my western shirts on display. I didn't make the shirt, but I did hand-embroider it. That shirt was basically my portfolio. That's what got me into the Swift Plant; it was the shirt I was wearing when I met the wife of the insurance agent who worked for the Swift Plant. At the boarding school, we would have elaborate horse shows at our commencements. I made all kinds of stuff for those events. Also, there at the museum is a serape that I made which went under the saddle, kind of like a banner that hangs down on each side of the horse. I also gave them one of my early *Arizona Farmer Ranchman* press passes, the one I used to get into the National Cattle Association Meeting. That press pass enabled me to get into meetings that were very expensive, with three-hundred-dollar registration fees. And I was getting into those meetings for free!"

Temple was at work, getting in the back door of things!

"Have you ever fallen off a horse, Temple?" I asked. "Once in high school," she responded, "and later, in my twenties, my aunt bought me a horse named Sizzler. Sizzler would buck when you changed gaits. He was perfect at the walk and trot, but when you'd ask him to canter, he'd start bucking. I fell off him three or four times. It wasn't any fun when that happened." But just like everything else, Temple got up, dusted herself off, and got back on the horse.

Photo of Temple's press pass, courtesy of The Cowgirl Hall of Fame Museum, Fort Worth, Texas

Chapter 8

"How often did you ride at the boarding school?" I wondered.

"When I was at the boarding school, we got to ride every afternoon. We didn't ride much in the winter because it was all snowy. When we couldn't ride, we skied! But even though I didn't ride in the winter, I still had to clean the barn. I can remember one year at Christmas when I went home, then came back, I found that no one had cleaned the stalls. The manure was frozen in the stalls, and I had to literally hack it out with a hoe. I was pretty mad. There were eight horses and a donkey, and it took me four hours to get all that frozen manure out!" This surely demonstrates Temple's sheer will and perseverance. She never quit. Just kept on going.

Temple went on to share this sad story, "In the movie, there was a horse that died, and that really happened. The reason it happened was because the school had bought oat straw instead of hay. I said to the riding instructor that it didn't look like hay, and asked if it was safe to feed to them. He said to go ahead and feed it to them. The biggest horse got colic from it and died. I can remember when the vet came, and asked me what I'd been feeding them. I showed him the horse feed, which was fine, but when I showed him the oat straw he had a fit! I told him that was what Mr. Davis told me to feed them. Shortly thereafter, they got regular hay again. Mr. Patey made it very clear that it was not my fault that this had happened—I did question the oat straw. I knew it didn't look like regular hay."

Temple knows that all her early days learning to work is what helped her later in life. She didn't have to transition to work as an adult because it happened gradually along the way, as it should for everyone. "I was very proud of the fact that I ran the horse barn. I was in charge of eight horses and the donkey, Jerry. So that was nine stalls. I did all the feeding; now, I didn't do any of the financials, but I did everything else. I'd hold each horse when the farrier came to do their feet, and help the vet when they came, just like in the movie when the big chestnut horse named Circus got sick. When I came down to the barn and found Circus leaning up against the wall in his stall, I went and found the riding instructor, Mr. Davis, and told him something was wrong. They called the vet to come out. Of course, there wasn't any internet back then that I could use to look up oat straw and see if it was safe for feeding. I felt really bad about the horse dying, but I was relieved that it wasn't my fault. They bought that because it was cheap. I did not choose that, that wasn't what I did at the barn. My job was to clean the stalls, bed the stalls, feed, put the horses out in the pasture, and when the farrier came, hold the horses for him. I pretty much did all that by myself."

Now picture Temple doing this: "We had a dairy barn at the school, and I learned how to milk cows by hand! It was a twelve-cow dairy, and we used those old-fashioned milk cans. We'd first clean the udders, then put the machine on them, and it would milk the cow. The milk would go into the milking machine, and we'd pour it into an old-fashioned milk jug. I remember once the power went out and we had to manually milk each cow. I really loved all the farm work."

Temple told me, "The other kids teased me, and they'd call me 'work horse' because I worked so hard. I'd be wearing my old jeans

Chapter 8

that had a patch on them. In the winter I'd be wearing a turtleneck, in the summer, shorts. Some of the other kids worked in the dairy barn, but when it came to those horse stalls, I was pretty much it! One of the things that made it really hard to bed the stalls was that I had to fill a bushel basket with the sawdust and carry it up the stairs, one bushel basket for each stall. It was a lot of work. Finally, we got a pully system so I could bring the sawdust up from the basement much easier." One question immediately came to mind, so I asked, "Did you design that pully system?" Temple replied, "Yes, I was involved in designing that!"

Temple realized that the other kids were not very interested in working hard like she did. "The other students did plenty of riding. My roommate did a lot of riding, we'd ride together, but she didn't do any of the stalls. None of the other students did any of the work, but they were right there to ride every day. I did everything. One thing I was always very careful to do was keep the lid closed on the grain bin. I was very, very careful to lock it and turn the latch." That way, in case a horse got loose during the night, they wouldn't be able to eat all the grain and get sick.

Even though Temple didn't study for those first three years at the boarding school, she was learning an even better skill that would take her very far. The skill of working hard. To this day, she still goes non-stop.

CHAPTER 9
Dating!

I'm quite sure that many people have wondered if Temple has ever had a boyfriend, or dated. Temple shared something with me that she's never told anyone. I guess she just felt comfortable to tell me.

"Temple, people want to know this: have you ever had a boyfriend, or dated anyone?" I asked. "Yes, there was one boy that I dated briefly while I was in college," she replied. "He was just a really nice guy, and we went out to Windows on the World at the World Trade Center. Everything was very nice, and we kissed once and that was it. I met him at college . . . I don't exactly remember if he was in a class, or what. He was about the same age as me. I can remember having a caesar salad up there at the top of the World Trade Tower in Windows on the World restaurant." That was one of the greatest restaurants New York City had ever seen. It was located on the one hundred and seventh floor of the World Trade Center, and it offered guests soaring views not only of Manhattan, but also Brooklyn and New Jersey. "I remember I wore a pretty dress, and he took me on our lovely evening for dinner," Temple stated. It's kind of like Temple Grandin à la reality TV!

"What a coincidence!" I told her, "I was up to that very restaurant back in my early twenties, around the same age as you were when you went there. I can remember I wanted to get right up near the windows and look out. How about you?" Temple gushed, "I loved looking out of the windows. That was the only guy I ever had an interest in or dated. I think he became a doctor, but I'm not sure. He was very nice, and very well-mannered. That was at Franklin Pierce College. It ended when I moved to Arizona."

I tried to delve deeper into the topic of when she dated the guy while at college. She declined any further discussion, stating that it wasn't a very deep relationship and it wasn't an important part of her life. Temple further added, "People are always looking for stuff that isn't important." I realize that to many people it is important. However, Temple is, without a doubt in my mind, a genius. A typical, mundane life certainly wouldn't suit someone of this magnitude. Temple had a bigger calling in life, one that ultimately helps millions of people around the globe. People might mistake her not pursuing such a relationship as a lack of caring or feeling. It's quite the opposite. Temple does a tremendous amount for others, and clearly demonstrates her depth of caring.

I'll share this with you. The other day I was talking to Temple's good friend Rosalie Winard, an author and Temple's photographer. I happened to mention this topic to Rosalie, and she was pretty surprised. She told me that Temple never told her about that guy she briefly dated in college. Then Rosalie said, "I remember something Temple once told me long ago regarding dating. She told me that when she was in college she saw her roommate fall for a guy, and her grades

Chapter 9

went from straight A's to rock bottom. The girl became obsessed with the guy and totally emotional, and couldn't focus on her studies any more. Temple said that when she saw that, she promised to herself that she'd never allow that to happen to her." I can easily see logical Temple stating that to herself.

I have my opinion about this topic. I've just got to say it. Temple has done great things with her life. She's helped millions of people, she loves what she does every day, and she has a sense of fulfilment most people will never know. She's experienced many exciting things. Had she gotten involved in a relationship, her life probably would not have gone where it did. I'm simply saying that relationships and marriage are not for everyone—on the spectrum, or neurotypical. I am extremely lucky for the great marriage I have, but I don't see that as the norm. With the divorce rate as high as it is, relationships can be either wonderful, or they can take a toll on a person. Temple has a number of individuals with whom she is very close, most of them for decades. They are there for her, and she shares her life with them. She leads a fulfilling life with a circle of close friends. That rocks! Way to go, Temple!

CHAPTER 10
Sports & Outdoor Activities

T emple participated in quite a number of sports in her younger days. For an individual with autism, that's very commendable. She was always out there doing something!

I found the following conversation pretty entertaining, as I was fascinated by ski jumping and always watch it during the winter Olympics. "What sports did you do, Temple?" Her response was, "There was the ski jump that the boys used in the winter time. I really wanted to do ski jumping, but I was too scared to try it. I just didn't have the balance. Even with simply skiing, I didn't have enough balance to stay upright and keep my feet together to do a nice 'christie.' But I could ski well enough that I enjoyed it, had fun, and at least I got out there and did it. I always watched ski jumping on the Olympics, and I wished I could do that."

Temple would have made a great ski jumper with her long legs!

"Do you enjoy being in snow?" I inquired.

"Oh yes, I loved being in the snow. I liked to ski, but I just couldn't get very far with it. I used to get so frustrated because no matter how many lessons I had, I just didn't get better. By the end of the winter, the other kids were skiing twice as well as me. There was a ski jump that people would use in the winter; they'd go on it and go about twenty feet up in the air! I really wanted to try it, so I did once, and I fell. I just didn't have the balance. But at least I did try it."

I don't think I'd have had the courage to even try doing it.

Temple shared, "I actually did a lot of sports. I was always a strong player—I could throw a ball really hard, I could kick hard. We played soccer in elementary school. Skiing, tennis, swimming, oh yes, I was out there doing it, and enjoying it all. I like to watch ski jumping during the winter Olympics, as well as gymnastics and extreme skateboarding. They go high up in the air! Some of that stuff I wouldn't be caught dead doing, but I like to watch it."

Still reminiscing about her younger days, Temple said "One of the things I loved to do as a kid was go skating on the pond. We played this game called 'crack the whip,' which you'd need about ten kids to do. There, again, I could only get to skate well enough to skate in a straight line, I couldn't do a figure eight or anything fancy. I was just too clumsy. But we also did a lot of sledding and tobogginng, and had a really good time doing all kinds of outdoor activities."

Oh, how fun! She continued, "We had a big box filled with scarves, bottle caps, hats, an old pipe, just old junk to decorate a snowman with, and that was our 'snowman box.' We had a system, where we'd each take turns. First, my sister would pick out a scarf, then I'd pick out a hat, then she'd pick out the eyes, and I'd pick out something for the mouth. That taught us turn taking." I just love it!

Chapter 10

Temple enjoyed so many sports! Here's more. "I used to play a lot of softball. I really liked that; back in elementary school, and the school in New Hampshire, we played it a lot. I could hit a ball hard and I had a strong arm, so I really enjoyed softball. The great thing was that there wasn't a lot of competition, we were just playing for fun and enjoying ourselves. Now, all the sports kids play are so competitive. That just wasn't the case back then."

All these things that Temple did, fun, child-like activities outdoors, were so critical in her development. All kids need to be out doing this kind of thing, but even more importantly, ASD kids need to be out there. These are the things that get them ready for their future. Temple said, "I really liked playing hopscotch on the pavement. We'd do that all the time, and draw the hopscotch board on the pavement with colored chalk. These were fun things we did with other kids. You simply had to do it with other kids, we didn't have the things to do by yourself like video games. You had to play with other kids!"

Like Temple and I always say, kids need to be outside just "doing stuff!" Temple was always outdoors. "We liked doing everything outside. We'd take the pods you get from a maple tree and make spinners out of them, or open the up at one end and stick it on your nose. We loved to play hide and seek. Everything was always outside."

Did you do stuff like this, too?

Making "Lots of Stuff"

Temple loved building and flying kites! She'll be the first one to tell you that. "Another thing I did as a young kid was making the kites and flying them. There was a small farm across the street that had a big field, it was called Kennedy's field, and we'd go there to fly the kites. It was those fifties-style kites, and it was a dime for the kite and a dime for the string. I got fifty cents a week for allowance. I spent a lot of time making my own kites, figuring out how to make them fly, then flying them as I rode my bicycle. I spent a lot of time making things. Kids don't make things anymore, which I think is very bad."

"Yes," I said, "all kids, not just those with autism, need to get out there and do active play. Just like kids used to do in the 'old days.'"

Learning to Ride a Bicycle

I asked her about learning to ride a bicycle, something quite daunting for most individuals with autism. "Temple, I'm curious about learning to ride a bicycle. It took me a very long time to get off the three-wheeler. How about you?" Her reply was, "That was pretty difficult for me because of my lack of balance. I was the last kid in the neighborhood to get off the trike. Then I got a small bike, and I'd try riding it across the lawn. I fell off of it plenty. I was slow to learn to ride it, but eventually I did. I initially had training wheels on it, but then those were taken off."

"One of the things that motivated me to learn to ride the bike was this group of kids, who were mentored by some parents. There was a trip to the soda bottling company, and it was a bike trip. I couldn't go

Chapter 10

because I couldn't ride my bike. Mother wouldn't take me there; she said I would have to learn to ride a bike. That was my biggest motivating factor. It was a year before I learned to ride my bike, because I just didn't have good balance. Eventually, once I was very proficient at bike riding, we'd do things like put play cards in the spokes to make a lot of noise as you pedal along. We would have bike races, and I'd be pedaling really fast, making a really loud noise, but then I suddenly realized that those cards were actually slowing me down. I also loved to fly a kite behind my bicycle as I went along really fast—I loved to do that!"

Once Temple learned to ride a bike, there was no stopping her. "We did a lot on our bikes. Long bike rides, racing them … in fact, I can remember just riding my bike to the pond, looking for flat stones, and skipping them on the pond. Just simple stuff like that. That's what kids did in the fifties. Another fun thing we did was get a bunch of empty tin cans and tie them on a string to the back of our bicycles, then ride all around the neighborhood. It made a racket!"

CHAPTER 11
Mother Nature

T emple loves the outdoors and beautiful scenery. She spent her whole youth outside, and her career choice takes her outdoors as well. I happened to think of the northern lights, and figured she would enjoy that as much as I do, so I asked her about it one day.

"Temple, have you ever seen the northern lights?"

"Yes, I saw the northern lights one time. We were driving in a car at night up in Canada, going to a cattle meeting. It was like seeing shimmering curtains moving. I'm pretty sure we were up in Alberta, traveling along a desolate country road. I could see them so clearly, and it was absolutely beautiful. I like to look at them online, as well." We continued talking about this for a while.

She went on, "I love being outside, especially in a huge pen with cattle. I like to sit down on the ground and have them all come up to me. They will come and surround you. It's really very peaceful. Just don't do it with bulls!" I had to ask, "Weren't you ever afraid that something would spook those cattle and they'd run you over?" "No, I never felt scared," Temple responded. Anyone who keeps up with Temple has probably seen the photos of her laying on the ground, surrounded by cattle. Those photos of Temple were taken by her friend Rosalie, who I mentioned earlier.

CHAPTER 12
Driving Miss Temple

The topic of driving related to those on the autism spectrum is a very serious one. It is not uncommon for individuals with autism to have great difficulty in learning to drive. They may take much longer to learn compared with their peers, or may never learn to drive at all. Temple pointed out that had she not learned to drive, she could not have pursued her career in the cattle industry. How would she have gotten around to all the cattle ranches and feed yards? Even if there was public transportation then like there is now, it still wouldn't have gotten her where she needed to go.

Parents need to understand that their ASD child will probably need a much longer period of time to master driving a vehicle. Even if it takes a year for them to learn to handle a car and feel comfortable and confident behind the wheel, safety is paramount. We simply learn differently than others.

"How old were you when you started learning to drive, Temple?" I asked. She replied, "I was about seventeen. My aunt Ann taught me how to drive on her ranch. It was three miles to the mailbox, and three miles back. By the end of the summer I had done over two hundred miles of driving before I went near any traffic. What I tell people at conferences about driving is that you need to burn up an entire tank of gas driving somewhere safe, where there's no traffic, before you go near any busy areas. Driver's education chucks them into it way too quickly. You need to learn how to operate the car first. I didn't realize how many miles I had driven—six miles a day, six days a week, that's thirty-six miles a week! Then, we started doing some real driving. We had to go through an old army fort to get into town. They didn't have learner's permits back then; I failed my first driver's test, but I passed my second one. Fortunately, on the army base, there wasn't any freeway driving or scary stuff like that. I went another year of driving before I was ready to drive on freeways. So, when I returned to college, I could drive around there because it was just easy roads with only a small amount of traffic. I can remember my first trip driving to New York. I planned a route that would be longer but have less traffic."

"So, what kind of driving can you do now—where are you able to go?" I asked. Temple said, "Now, I can drive everywhere. I hate going to downtown Denver because the roads are designed so poorly. I like to stay in the right-hand lane and go slow. But in Denver, if you stay in the right-hand lane, you get pushed off the exits! You have to do a lot of lane-changing to get into the middle lane to get past the exits. I just don't like that! I try to time my trips into Denver to avoid the rush hour. When I'm going to the airport, I turn off on a toll road just before the airport to avoid a lot of traffic. I know every inch of the road along the whole route to the airport. Then, I have my special area I park in at the Denver International Airport parking lot. There's typically a lot of empty spaces in this particular area."

"Wow!" I started, "I know you have to go to the airport multiple times each week. That's a lot."

Temple reiterated her advice for learning to drive, "When it comes to driving, I highly recommend practicing in a totally safe place, like an empty parking lot, quiet roads, or an open field. You've got to totally learn how to operate that vehicle before you can go where there's any traffic! It has to become a motor function before you can safely drive out on busy roads."

"I totally agree. Absolutely," I added.

Laughing, Temple shared, "I had to learn on a horrible clutch! So, Ann did something really clever. One day, when we were going to the mailbox, she said to slide over and just steer. So, for five or six trips to the mailbox all I did was steer, and she handled the horrible clutch. Then she got me down at the base of the driveway where there was nothing to hit. Boy, that truck lurched and jumped at first!"

"Of course," she went on, "I never text while I'm driving, or do anything that's distracting. Just focus on the driving!"

Listen to Temple, everyone! We need to make baseball caps and T-shirts that say, "What Would Temple Do?"

Here's more from Temple. "I stress the importance of learning how to drive. It enabled me to have my career! If I didn't drive, I would never have been able to achieve success in my career. I wouldn't have been able to go to all the feed yards and processing plants. You just have to do it. I highly suggest getting the learner's permit, and learning to drive slowly. Do a little more each week, and gradually build up the skills. Driving is something you don't jump into the deep end with. It must be a slow process. I think we must get more proactive on finishing the transition before they graduate from high school. Shopping. Bills. Laundry. Driving. A job."

The individual with autism and their family need to understand that it's going to take a lot of time to fully learn to handle the vehicle and feel comfortable to drive. Patience is necessary. Be happy with every small step, they eventually add up to giant steps.

While out on the roads driving, everyone experiences something that gets their heart pounding, and perhaps a few colorful words blurted out! Temple is just like everyone else. She shared this scary experience with me when I asked, "Temple, has there ever been anything scary that happened while you were driving?" She replied, "Once while driving, a board came flying across the road—that was scary as hell. I was in the right-hand lane on the freeway, minding my own business, and a car passed me with a little low trailer on the back that had no tailgate. There were three two-by-sixes on it. Then he passes me, and just as he does, the board slides off. I remember locking onto it like a fighter jet radar and my visual took over. This board was floating on a diagonal angle right toward me. I followed that board and eased over to my right into the breakdown lane, and I did a perfect job of straddling it. The second I straddled that board, my heart started pounding and every swear word I could think of came out of me to describe the trailer, the board, and the driver! It took me about twenty minutes to calm down."

Don't you just love it, swear words and all?

CHAPTER 13
Work Hard to Succeed

S omething that came up multiple times throughout our conversations was regarding the fact that she comes from a wealthy family. She'd see it in print, or people would say it throughout her whole life. She said she's seen it online that people have bashed her about coming from a wealthy family. It truly hurts her feelings. While it was true that Temple's family had money, that isn't the reason she is where she is today. What got her to this point is her extreme intelligence, perseverance, and endless hard work. One day while talking, Temple was very happy to learn that I came from a very poor family. She then started saying, "You are proof that it can be done having come from a poor family! I want you to include something in this book telling people about all the jobs you did when you were young. All of that built the skills necessary for success as an adult. You are proof that a person with autism who came from a poor family can be successful! I think this is really exciting, and people need to see this." Temple asked how I afforded to attend college. I told her I had to take out over one hundred thousand dollars in student loans, which took me over ten years to pay off. Temple's response was, "This needs to be in the book, people need to see this. All those childhood jobs enabled you to have a successful career as an adult. It was a lot of hard work, but you did it. It was all early exposure!" At the end of this book, I have included a bit of what Temple asked me to share with you. It's in the afterword.

"Temple, what was your biggest motivating factor to work as hard as you did?" I asked. She continued, "When I was in my twenties, my motivating factor was to prove I wasn't dumb. There were a lot of people who didn't think I was going to amount to anything. So when I designed those dip vats and I did the drawings for the Red River project, when I completed the drawings and I looked at them, I couldn't believe I had done them. I didn't think I had it in me to do it. Proving that I could do it was a big thing. Yes, I had the love of the cattle, but I had a really big motivation that I could really do something! I did not do that dip vat because I had to survive. I did it because I wanted to. That's what made me design all my cattle facilities—because I wanted to do them. I wanted to prove that I could do it. It also allowed me to use my mind to solve problems."

Temple has very artistic talents, which later in life enabled her to draw her elaborate designs for the cattle facilities. In boarding school, she started demonstrating these talents by painting signs. She explains, "In the sixties and seventies, signs were hand-painted on plywood. My first sign was for a beauty shop. I hand painted the name of it on the sign, it was 'Virginia's Beauty Shop.' I was about seventeen, so I made these signs in my room at the boarding school. I had made friends with one of the carpenters working on the building, and it was his wife who owned the beauty shop. He asked me to paint it and handed me a ten-dollar bill!" Temple loves talking about the sign painting gig! Don't you just love the photo of her by the white truck?

Photo courtesy of Temple Grandin

"Where did you get that white truck?" I asked. "I had a white Ford Ranger that I used for my sign painting business. This was one time it certainly helped coming from a wealthy family. I had walked into the car dealership and went into the truck area, and they didn't even want to pay attention to me. So, I went over to the car area, and said I wanted to buy a pickup. Nobody would hardly even look at me. I then asked how much it was, and I wrote out a check for it. They about dropped their teeth! So, in that situation I was lucky to come from a wealthy family and be able to do that. I know that they thought I was just so weird that I could possibly be interested in buying a truck. When

I bought it, the car salesman got the commission, because the truck salesman didn't give me the time of day. They couldn't believe when I pulled out the check and wrote it out for the entire cost." Sadly, those on the spectrum have probably all experienced something like that out in public, getting ignored like that. I would have loved to hear what went on at that dealership after she left.

Temple continued, "You get better and better by getting out there and doing things, adding data to your data base. When you sit there all day playing video games, you're not adding anything to your data base! I also think I learned to be brazen by helping out at my mother's dinner parties, because I had to go up to each person and greet them, take their coats, and all that. I had a sewing job when I was thirteen, then I'd take people out on trail rides at my aunt's ranch. I'd wait on tables, and did internships in college. I had my sign painting business. That's where I first started to learn to work. Like you, when you wanted to do something, you went and did it. That's the 'can do' attitude. People don't have that today."

I asked Temple for more details on her summer internships. They would have been great for any college student, but they were even better for a person with autism; it got her interacting with people and working. Here's what Temple told me. "I worked in a research lab one summer where they did pharmaceutical experiments on mice, and I had to run the experiments. They wanted to see how alcohol interacted with antidepressants. So, I'd inject mice with some alcohol and antidepressants, put them on their backs, and see how long

Chapter 13

it took them to wake up and right themselves. It was like a regular job, in that I had to be there from eight in the morning to five in the evening every day. Then, there was another internship at a hospital that Mother set up. They had kids with autism there, and I was assigned to be a one-on-one aid to a little girl who was nonverbal. She was terrified of elevators. They had rickety old wooden elevators, and she was afraid the doors had wooden arms that would catch her. It was ancient, like a 1930s elevator. My job was just to stay with the little girl the whole time. When the other kids did a group game, I'd be involved in that, too."

"Where did you live while you were doing the internship?" I inquired. "I was supposed to live in a house they had on the grounds, but that went under construction, so at the last minute I had to find a room to rent. I talked to the other staff members, and they found a room I could rent in a house. So, I was doing a lot of stuff on my own. This was in the sixties."

Temple continued, "See, when I did the other internship at the research lab, I rented a house with another woman. Somebody at the college had set that up, as they had a friend who knew the woman. So, I ended up renting a room at her house and paying her rent." Curious, I asked, "How did you contend with a strange person?" Temple replied, "I was renting a house with a new person, and driving to all my jobs—very independent things. I got to do some other fun things while I was there. Someone had a motorcycle and I figured out how to make a burglar alarm for it. If somebody moved the motorcycle, the horn would go off. It was really simple, a mercury switch, so when you tilt it, it goes off. I was so happy when I made that work," she laughed.

Temple can always find some new adventure. "Another fun thing I got to do there, was the only time I ever got to wear a scuba outfit and go in the pool. I swam around in the pool with the scuba outfit on, and the sensation of breathing underwater was really weird."

"Were you getting paid at those jobs?" I asked. Temple replied, "Both those internships were unpaid. Mother set that up through her contacts. That was at a hospital in Providence, Rhode Island. The research lab was at the Worchester Foundation for Experimental Biology. That was set up by a woman on campus who knew someone there. Mother got me doing those really independent things. The third summer she only let me stay at my aunt's ranch for four weeks, then I went to do those internships. The first two summers I spent the entire time at my aunt's ranch. Mother wanted me to experience more, learn new things, and interact with other people."

"Well, how did you feel about going somewhere new like that?" I asked.

"You see, my mother wanted me to do something else. She said to me, 'We need you to try to learn some other things.' So, I only did the ranch for half the summer. She didn't just take the ranch away. There were two and a half months of summer, so I did four weeks at the ranch and the rest at the internships. I was interested in going for the challenge of it, and I did it. It forced me to do a lot of things independently."

Chapter 13

I commented, "It's a pretty big deal for a kid with autism to have done all that, to go and be with total strangers and have to get along. What did you do while you were renting the room at the lady's house? Did you interact much with her?"

"Oh yeah, we did," she told me. "We went to see *Chitty Chitty Bang Bang* together. Afterward, she wanted to have liver for dinner, and I wanted to make sure it was cooked enough to not get trichomonas from it." She paused here to laugh at the memory. "So we went out and got the liver, then got a cookbook and looked it up to be sure we cooked it enough!" Temple was laughing heartedly reminiscing that escapade. Temple wasn't much on parties, but I'm not surprised she went to this one: "One weekend, the foundation had a scientist party, and I went to that." See what I mean? She knew there'd be a room full of scientists. It probably reminded her of back in the day, sitting with her grandfather on Sunday afternoons.

As you can see, Temple was always out there doing something. And that's why she is where she is today. A person simply cannot stay home on their computer, not working, not interacting with others, not learning how to live. There's no getting around it. One has to start at a young age. Like Temple said earlier, she wants to get away from the "transition to work." If it's been being done all along, there wouldn't be a transition, simply a progression.

CHAPTER 14
Things That Make Temple Cry

The general public is under the misconception that individuals with autism don't have any feelings or emotions because there's typically a lack of facial expressions. Remember in the introduction, when I talked about the saying "still water runs deep?" Well, that really applies to those of us on the autism spectrum. Temple experiences sadness, too, and I'll share those things here.

Temple talked about crying, and I asked, "Did you have anyone who you'd call when you were upset?" She replied, "When I'd get upset, I'd go cry somewhere. I had people that'd I'd call for emotional support, yes. I'd call Ann at the ranch. I'd talk to Jim the contractor about things. There were people like Jim that were good to me."

The summer Temple spent at her aunt's ranch changed her life forever. Of course, Temple developed a special kinship with Ann during that time. I could sense it was painful for Temple to answer these questions, but I felt I needed to ask them. "Temple, I need to ask you these questions. How did you feel when you lost people who were important to you?" Temple replied, "I can remember when my aunt Ann died. That was extremely sad. That happened in the late eighties. I went and visited her, and she was almost like a skeleton. I can remember walking around in this shopping center like a zombie, I just couldn't believe it. I went back and saw her one more time, and then I left. She looked absolutely awful. I can't remember what she died of, but I remember she was all shriveled up and weak. That was extremely sad."

I then asked, "When your Aunt finally did die, how did you cope with that?" Temple's voice changed when she answered this question. "Well, what was really awful was seeing her right on death's doorstep. That was worse than finding out that she died."

I remembered her talking about her relationship with Oliver Sacks, so I asked, "What about when Oliver Sacks died?" Temple went on, "I can remember reading in the *New York Times* about Oliver Sack's life on the computer in my kitchen, and crying so hard I couldn't work the computer. I used to go over Oliver's home every year, a few days before or a few days after Christmas." When I talked to Temple's friend Rosalie Winard, she told me that she also went with Temple to visit Oliver. She took lots of photos of Temple at their gatherings. Temple went on, "Oliver always talked about which way he could have gone in life. There was an editorial he wrote before he died, it was in the *New York Times*, but I was so upset that I couldn't work the computer right. When I'd go to visit, we'd usually go out to dinner and then to his place for a bit and we'd talk. The editorial that he wrote was about the meaning of life, and it was right before he died. He knew he was going to die. He talked about the different ways his life could have gone." Curious to hear it, I asked, "What were the ways it could have gone?" Temple stated, "Well, he could have gone into a very religious way of life, and the other way was writing. You know, circumstances determine where you go. Yeah, that was extremely sad. Then I wrote something about him for a documentary."

Temple called me with one last thing to add in this chapter. She started, "When I get asked about religion, I think of my Hubble Deep Space Field picture, which I've had for the last fifteen years or so. It just shows hundreds of galaxies; not stars, galaxies! I look at that, and that's what makes me think about religion. You know, there's a big universe out there." I could hear Temple's voice get a bit shaky. She continued, "The little badge they made for me at Cape Kennedy, I hung that on the deep space field poster. That's where it belongs. I get to thinking about the time I stood in front of the vehicle assembly building at NASA, and ask myself why we do something like go to the moon. It's a search for knowledge." I added, "Well, when I look at photos from the Hubble, I start pondering where it begins, where it ends, and how it all started." Temple replied, "We don't know. We just don't know. That's why they use the Hubble to seek answers."

"So, elaborate more on your thoughts about religion when you look at that Hubble Deep Space Field image," I prompted. She replied, "I think about the great unanswered questions. Why are we here, what's out there? I don't know. Nobody knows. When I was younger, I'd wonder what the meaning of life is. I was just at several autism conferences, where families come up to me and tell me that my advice changed their child's life. That's a very positive thing in my life, and I think that gives it a lot of meaning. I did something earlier today when I was sitting at the airport in Milwaukee; a parent came up to talk to me with her very shy daughter. I asked the girl if she had ever done any shopping on her own. She started squirming a little and looking around. I took out a five-dollar bill and handed it to her and said, 'Go over to that news stand and buy yourself something,' pointing right across the walkway to the stand. While the girl walked over to buy something, the mother remained by me and admitted that she babies the girl."

I blurted out, "Oh, I love that idea that you did that! I think it's really great!" Temple added, "The girl returned and gave me the change. She bought a soda. I just wanted her to experience shopping for something and buying it on her own! This kid was fourteen years old." I replied, "She will always remember that!"

Just in case you are not up on astronomy, the Hubble Space Telescope is a space telescope that was launched into low Earth orbit in 1990 and remains in operation. Although it is not the first space telescope, Hubble is one of the largest and most versatile, and is well known as both a vital research tool and a public relations boon for astronomy. It is named after the astronomer Edwin Hubble, and is one of NASA's Great Observatories.

Temple shared, "My trip to the Kennedy Space Center was really emotional for me when I saw a Space X launch. The museum they have there at the visitor's center was really nice, too. They had an exhibit there about astronauts who have died, and that was done extremely well."

Chapter 14

There is No Single Turning Point

"Temple, what was the most profound thing that happened in your life?" I inquired.

"People are always asking me that, looking for a single turning point. It's more like a series of doors. I think the first thing would be Mother getting me into the nursery school and speech therapy school. When I talked to her about that, she said they spent a lot of time with us, sitting at a table learning how to take turns. That was a big part of the therapy. There were five or six other little kids, and you had to learn how to wait and take turns along with the speech therapy."

Dealing with Setbacks

This topic garners a lot of emotion out of Temple. "One of the things that made me cry was getting kicked out of Scottsdale feed yard. The way I dealt with that was to go right down to the *Arizona Farmer Ranchman* magazine office and ask if I could write a column. I had to replace crying with taking decisive action. My way to retaliate the Scottsdale feed yard was get a press pass so they would have to let me in."

Continuing, Temple stated, "I've had lots of situations that failed, and I picked myself up and dealt with it. There were some times I dealt with it on my own, and sometimes there were people to help me. I can remember when I had a skin cancer that they had to take off my eye lid and it took a really long time to heal, and I got really big nerve attacks with that. It was before I took the antidepressants. There was a really nice lady named Penny Porter that I visited; she also had some bad eye problems, so we could relate on that. I was really nervous about that because I was worried something could go wrong and I'd go blind. I was in my late twenties, and it was a basal cell carcinoma right on the margin of my eyelid. It had to be done while I was awake, with only lidocaine local anesthetic injected all around my eye. It was no fun watching the knife coming right by my eye. I smelled the cauterizing and saw everything. I actually went through the surgery fine, but had trouble with the healing. Of course, I have a tendency towards anxiety attacks, but I remember going to visit Penny Porter at her ranch and she was very supportive. She had some bad glaucoma problems with her eyes. I can remember her saying over and over not to worry, that I was going to get over it. It took about three weeks to a month to finally heal up."

Temple has had her share of ups and downs on the job, just like everyone else. "I got upset at a job I was working on in the early nineties; there was an awful plant manager. There was a lot of sexism, and I got kicked out of the plant. I hadn't done anything wrong. I can remember getting really, really upset about that. I knew I didn't do anything wrong, but it was all about this nerd girl coming into their territory. What made me keep going was this message I remembered that had been written on the wall at Arizona State University: 'Obstacles are those frightful things you see when you take your eyes off the goal.' I have since learned that Henry Ford wrote that." This has now become one of my favorite quotes!

Among all her successes, how did Temple deal with failures? "I had a job in 1980 that failed. They wanted to make a conveyer belt that would take pigs up to the third floor, and all it did was flip them over backwards. It was a real mess. What I learned from that was to treat causes of problems, and not just symptoms. Probably if we had changed the pig's genetics, they would have been able to walk up the ramp just fine. I got really upset at that. It was my first project failure. From that, I learned that engineering cannot fix bad pig genetics. I learned to look at the root cause of a problem."

"How did you deal with such things?" I asked. "What helped me deal was having more than one project going at a time. If something fails, you know … don't put all your eggs in one basket." I then stated that was an idiomatic expression, and asked how she learned them. "You just have to have them explained. Well, each job is like an egg. I went to some seminars when I was first starting my business and they were extremely helpful. One of the things they taught me at a consulting seminar at the American Society of Agricultural Consultants was never to sign a no-compete clause, and make sure you have more than one client. That way, if something fails, you have other projects. Someone at the seminar used the term 'don't put all your eggs in one basket.' I asked someone to explain it to me, so they said it meant not to just have one big client, but have many, so that if one drops you, you still have other clients. I can visualize that if you drop the basket, all your eggs will break. I find myself using idioms all the time because I can visualize them. I particularly like the sayings 'you need to have more than one iron on the fire,' and 'strike when the iron is hot.' I learned these at those seminars. The first thing I did was join the American

Society of Agricultural Consultants. In fact, I was the first woman to ever be on their board." See, Temple made some great business moves, like attending those seminars for advice. Quite the savvy young lady, I must say!

"Tell me about your very first speaking engagement, Temple," I stated.

"I got invited to do a paper for the American Society of Agricultural Engineers in December of 1974, where I presented some of my cattle-handling work. That was my very first talk. I'll always remember that. It was at a hotel in Chicago. My presentation was about basic cattle handling: things like distractions, what worked, what didn't, and shadows. I had really great slides for that, because I had consulted with an engineer who advised me not to just focus on the negative things. Focus on the positive. It really worked."

As Temple was talking to me about her first presentation, she was in a hotel room that had pillows with duck down, which she's allergic to. I kept hearing her sniffling, and I thought she was coming down with a cold. Then she told me she was having the room de-feathered! She was sniffling and sneezing throughout the entire conversation. Sneezing again, Temple said, "They took the feathers out, but there's still feather cooties in here." I haven't heard the word "cooties" in quite some time, and I loved it! It needs to become the new buzz word. I asked her how could she be around farm animals but be allergic to feathers. She said it was only duck down that stirred up the allergy. So, don't send Temple any duck down pillows as a gift!

Chapter 14

The Good Things That Made Temple Cry

We got to talking again about her days in elementary school when her mother, Eustacia, organized plays for the fair each year, and the time *The Wizard of Oz* was done. Temple wasn't in that play, but watched it being performed. I asked Temple if she liked to watch the TV movie *The Wizard of Oz*. "I loved it, absolutely loved it. I always used to cry about the ruby slippers getting her back home. It's sort of like, and this is something that makes me cry, she had the ruby slippers but she didn't know she had the power in them. I still get choked up about that." I heard Temple start to cry, and I was already crying, too. I said, "I understand that. It's like a person has a gift but they don't understand how to use it." Temple sniffed, "That's right, she just didn't know how to use them. I can't even think about it without getting teary." I muttered, "I know I have a gift, but I haven't figured out how to use it yet."

Temple said, "Well, helping kids become successful is one way you can do that. That's one of the things I get to help people with. Every time I think about Dorothy with her red slippers, it's like the door is right there but she doesn't see it. But, with all my career opportunities, I did see the door. I did walk right up to that editor and ask him for his card, just like the movie showed. I did that scene. That goes back to being taught party hostess when I was a little kid, I had to greet each guest then serve snacks. One thing I learned very early is that certain people can open the door. Now the parents are too into the medical model, and they don't even see the door." We both continued to cry and talk. It was pretty emotional. Now I can't wait to see *The*

Wizard of Oz again soon. I'm betting it will look a little different this time around.

There was something back from her childhood days that Temple recalled. "Here's something that made me really sad. I used to like *Howdy Doody*. I can remember the back of the boxes of Blue Bonnet margarine when they had these cut-outs of all the *Howdy Doody* characters, and I wanted to collect them all to get the *Howdy Doody* stage. Mother said we couldn't get the stage until we bought enough margarine to get all of the characters. I very carefully got all ten characters. Then I sent my fifty cents in, and about a month or six weeks later I got my fifty cents back and a letter saying, 'We're very sorry, but we ran out of stages.' That was a situation where Mother wanted to teach me that you need to get all your figures first. I remembered that each week we'd get another box of Blue Bonnet margarine, and I'd carefully cut out the figure. When I finally had all ten figures, I sent my fifty cents in. Mother was trying to teach me how to wait, but we waited too long, and they were out of *Howdy Doody* stages."

As you can see, Temple has emotions and feelings just like everyone else does. Everyone on the autism spectrum has them. We might not show it like others do, but that doesn't mean they're not there.

CHAPTER 15
Temple's Dream Vacation—Total NASA Geek-Out

When I asked Temple what her dream vacation would be (if she actually had time to take one!), I sort of knew what she'd say before she answered. I knew it wasn't going to be on a cruise to the Bahamas. Can you guess before reading on?

"Okay, Temple," I started, "so what would be your idea of a dream vacation?"

Temple jumped at this question, "I think it would be really exciting to go to the International Space Station! I've been to NASA, and seeing everything there was a lot of fun! I've been to quite a few places at NASA: I've been to the Jet Propulsion Lab, I've been to the Control Room in Houston. When I first entered the Control Room, it was empty. I then learned that as the Space Station goes around, they have blackouts because there are places where they have no communication. That's when everyone goes to the bathroom. It's kind of like those places on the highway where you know your phone is going to go out; there's a certain time of the day when they know the Space Station will have no communication. But then everyone came back in, and they were fully working."

Temple was quite beside herself! She was on a roll, "They have a Space Station mock-up. One of the astronauts told me that I ask really good questions. We were in a space shuttle mockup and were looking out the window at the cargo bay, and there was a switch, similar to a light switch, that said 'pyro.' I noted, 'That's not a switch you'd want to touch accidentally,' and he responded, 'Yes, you wouldn't want to touch that, because it would blow the cargo out of the cargo bay!' I asked why it didn't have a guard over it. They were interested that I noticed that sort of thing. I did get to put a spacesuit glove on, and it's like a big clumsy heavy winter glove. Going to the International Space Station (ISS) is my idea of my dream vacation! And going on a spacewalk. I know that's totally out of the question, but I can fantasize!" I'll tell you that Temple was really buzzed up talking about this, like a little kid on Christmas morning!

Temple asked me, "Have you ever been to the Chicago airport in the United concourse? They have these tunnels that have neon lights in it. I can remember when they first built it in the early eighties, and I walked through it, thinking to myself, 'This is about as close I'm going to get to *Star Trek*.' I'd walk through that tunnel, imagining that I was on a space station somewhere! I was like, 'Oh, wow! This is super cool!'" I immediately looked up the United concourse at Chicago's O'Hare International Airport. Sure enough, there it was. Go check it out. You can then picture Temple strolling along in seventh heaven!

Aside from space, Temple had another vacation spot she'd love to go. "I'd also love to visit an off-shore oil rig! I think that would be really fun. I can remember reading all about how oil rigs operate, and it was claimed that it's as complicated as going to the moon."

I'm doubting this one's on a vacation website.

Oh boy. I knew she was wound up, so I just continued to listen. She went on, "I get thrilled by inventive things people have done. Let me tell you something exciting about the Mars Rover; this makes me happy!" She chuckled. "They had to design the wheels with a marker to signify each time they made a full revolution. They designed it so the marker was Morse code for the Jet Propulsion Lab! I thought that was totally funny."

Seeing a Real Rocket Launch is More Exciting than a Video

Temple had just returned from a visit to NASA (early October 2017) to give a talk on disability and she called me up to share in her excitement. Now, I'm sharing it with you! Temple gushed, "I got invited down to NASA to give a talk on disability to their employees with disabilities. I did a TED-type talk. I got to go on the coolest tour; I got to see a Space X launch! I can tell you, seeing a real launch is not the same thing as seeing it on television. Right before the launch, a helicopter flew over the area to be sure no one was in the danger zone, and we were right on the edge of the legal zone. We had a pass, and got in as close as anyone was allowed. It was really loud! Very different than on TV. They had a smart phone there so you could listen to the countdown. And let me tell you about the NASA Launch Control Center! They told me that you know the launch is going well when they start to fiddle with the adjustments on their chairs!"

"I got to go into the vehicle assembly building, and on the roof of the vehicle assembly building. That really made me think about the fact that that the astronauts have the right stuff to fly in the rockets, but the geeks make the stuff. ('Make sure you put that in the book,' she told me, 'that's my new saying!') Then, I got to go on a mobile launch pad that will go on a crawler road for the Mars mission. It had a big banner that said 'The Future is Here with a trip to Mars' and an American flag on it. As I walked into it, I got to thinking: an Asperger kid needs to be building this, not playing video games in the basement. When we arrived at that building, we almost parked in Elon Musk's parking lot at the SpaceX parking lot. There were only about fifty cars there."

You know who Elon Musk is, right? If you don't, go look him up. Temple has already read his biography and keeps up with everything he's doing. There's also a great article on him in *Rolling Stone*! I've now become a big Elon Musk fan, too!

Boy, Temple sure livens up when she starts talking about NASA! I could easily picture her commanding a flight to the International Space Station. Temple continued, "When I went to NASA, I met an Astronaut named Rick Linnehan. We talked about the robotic hand, and the spacesuit glove." Temple had read that the Russian astronaut, the cosmonaut that did an early spacewalk, got into a lot of trouble because they didn't design the spacesuit right. "It got over-inflated and his hands pulled out of the gloves and his feet pulled out of the boots. I thought, 'You've got to be kidding. That thing should have been tested in a vacuum chamber!' I was really surprised at that. He had to let

Chapter 15

some of the air out of the suit so he could move and fit back into the chamber. That's a really bad visualization mistake."

Temple's voice started wavering, as it does when she gets very emotional. "As I stood in front of the vehicle assembly building, I got all choked up thinking about how we did something really special when we did this. We went to the moon, and we did it without sophisticated technology. It blew my mind when I found out that the Gemini and Mercury flights were hand-calculated. I want to read more about the spacesuit and Playtex's involvement in that, because the bra seamstresses that sewed them never got any credit. You see, a bra company would know how to design something so that the hands and feet wouldn't pull out—that's what I was thinking about while I was reading about the Russian cosmonaut. There he was, enjoying his spacewalk, then his spacesuit starts overinflating. He might not fit back into the hatch, and his hands were no longer in the gloves. Thank goodness he didn't panic, or else he'd have been dead. This is something the visual thinker would have seen; I would have been yelling to test it out in a vacuum chamber. The engineering mind just doesn't see that. I think this just comes down to different kinds of minds! In his book, *Spacesuit*, Nicholas de Monchaux wrote about the huge culture clash between the people at Playtex and the engineers. I am almost sure that the visual thinkers at Playtex and the mathematical engineers did not understand each other."

She continued, "I read about the head designer at Playtex, and I remember one line that I thought was really funny. They said one pipe from the tank went to the girdle factory and the other went to the spacesuit line, and they put the best bra seamstresses on it. Those seamstresses never got any credit, but if they didn't do it correctly the astronauts would have died. The designers at Playtex had no degrees, they have graduated from the 'school of hard knocks.'"

I had to share this with Temple, "I had the opportunity to meet two astronauts back in 2001: Commander Robert "Copa" Cabana, and Commander Wendy Lawrence. They had both just returned from the International Space Station. I asked them the most profound part of their experience, and they both said the moment they were up in space, looked out the window, and saw the Earth. They also described the launch and what that felt like. I can remember I reached over, asking them both if I could touch them! They laughed and said yes. I touched them lightly on their shoulder. I got goosebumps! Just knowing these two people were up in the International Space Station was mind-boggling."

Reminiscing about her younger days, Temple said, "I can remember the moon landing, and going out in the back yard and looking up on the moon and saying, 'There's people up there, walking around.' That was when I was in college, during the summer I was living in a rental house with a roommate and doing my internships."

A New Perspective of Earth

Temple was still excited, "I'll never forget those pictures that show the Earth as a blue marble floating in space. It gives you a totally different view of our planet. I can remember I was in high school, just starting at the Hampshire school, when the Mercury Seven group was formed. When I was young, it was something that seemed so far away … I couldn't even imagine being allowed doing something like that."

"My Cape Kennedy trip had the most profound effect on me. I stood there looking at the vehicle assembly building and thinking about what we accomplished. I get all choked up at Kennedy's speech, 'We choose to go to the moon in this decade and do other things, not because they are easy, but because they are hard.' When you look at the technology we have, when I went inside the launch platform, the kind of piping and gauges they're using even now look like something out of Jules Verne. When I looked inside, there was so much iron work. I realize they had to assemble the rocket upright because it was so heavy. They still use materials that looks like they're out of an antique shop because it's very reliable, and with rocket fuel you need really reliable. It's not the place to experiment."

Okay. Do you know who Jules Verne is?

I was in a store the other day and saw a *National Geographic* magazine all about astronauts, so I got one for Temple and one for myself. I sent it right out to her, but since I'm finishing up this book I didn't have time to even touch my copy. No worries. Temple is telling me every detail of all the articles in the book. She got a case of the giggles as she shared with me the part about the Russian cosmonauts who took vodka into space with them, and the astronaut who decided to take a pastrami sandwich with him to eat once in space. I do hope he ate it before it spoiled. I'm soon to know every last detail about spacesuits, as I've just sent her an early Christmas gift of two books she mentioned about them.

Temple and I talked a lot about NASA and spacesuits. This is one of her big passions. I guess she's got me into it, too, as I had the craziest dream the other night. I dreamt that Temple, myself, and Elon Musk were at NASA at midnight, going around inside the buildings and playing with all the rockets and equipment. It was like the opening scene

Photo courtesy of Temple Grandin

Photo courtesy of Temple Grandin

Photo courtesy of Temple Grandin

CHAPTER 16
Fear of Flying

Temple is walking into an airplane three, four, sometimes five times a week! Now she sleeps during flights, or catches up on reading. No more white knuckles.

"When I was in my twenties, I was really scared to fly. There was a situation where we had to make an emergency landing, and it took me about three years to get over that. I was a white-knuckle flyer during those years!" I asked, "How do you go from white-knuckle flyer to all the time you now spend in airplanes?" Her reply was, "I had to make planes go from scary to interesting, so I learned all about how planes work." There's that logical side surfacing again.

"Here's what happened. It was my third flight. I was coming home from the ranch, and a jet airplane was still a novelty. That was my first time flying alone. My first flight was with my roommate, the second time I flew with my aunt, but the third time I was by myself. I was actually having fun, listening to the music and anticipating being served my meal. Back then, everyone dressed up in really nice clothes to go on a plane. I had on a white flowered summer dress; I had to wear dresses to go on a plane! And there were headphones that were like a stethoscope to listen to music while flying. I was sitting on the right side of the plane, about three quarters of the way back. The next thing I know, the plane lurches to the side while we're at thirty thousand feet. We were over Kansas when it happened, and we ended up landing in Salina, Kansas. The plane lurched to the right, and all the trays flew up into the air. They hadn't served me yet, only half the plane had been served. The flight attendants started throwing the trays on the floor and yelling for everyone to put their seatbelts on, and to prepare for emergency landing. Emergency landing! The plane was then descending really fast, and we had no explanation for what was going on. I was sure I was going to die. We landed with the pilot jamming on the brakes and fish-tailing down the runway. The plane stopped, and the doors opened to the slide chutes being deployed. The flight attendants started yelling, 'Abandon plane! Abandon plane! There's a bomb on the plane! Once you hit the ground, start running and don't look back! Just keep running!'"

Temple's voice was all excited as she went on, "That was back in the day when there was no overhead storage bin, just a shelf. I had my bag with me that I had my cameras in, my two prized possessions. They grabbed it out of my hands and flung it into the galley. I jumped out of the door and down the slide I went; then I ran. Finally, we were all standing around, and the pilot told me there was a woman on the plane who had looked at her watch at was ten minutes to two. She said, 'At two o'clock, we're all going to die. And I don't know which bag they put my bomb in!' So, the pilot thought he had ten minutes to get on the ground from cruising altitude."

Chapter 16

"They started unloading the baggage, but they didn't have the equipment to get it all off. Then they just started shoving it all out of the aircraft, crashing to the ground. They finally found her bag, and the bomb squad came and took it away. Then they took her carry-on bag and threw it into a ditch. They decided to go through all the bags in one of the hangars. I was standing next to a man who had a brief-case, and when he opened it up there were some weird electronics in it. Security wanted to tear it all apart. He started hollering, 'No, please don't do that! I'm a salesman for luminescent light bulbs and this is my demonstrator!'"

"I'm sure everyone was pretty jumpy at that point! No wonder they freaked out!" I added.

Temple shared the rest of the story, "And then we had to go back on the airplane and get our belongings, which had been thrown in the galley. Back then carry-on bags weren't allowed, only coats, hats, and purses. They had taken every purse and dumped it out in the galley, so everyone was going through all of it to find their stuff. I was able to find my things, including my two cameras. Then they brought another plane in from Chicago. I got back on, but then after that I was totally scared when I had to fly."

Aviation went from Scary, to Interesting

"So, tell me how you got over that?" I asked. Temple said, "By making airplanes go from scary to interesting. I had a chance in the early seventies to go to a meeting called the Animal Air Transportation

Association. I got to go to their cargo area down in Miami, and travel on their constellation (the 'Cow S—t Connie') to Puerto Rico with a plane load of heifers. They had holes drilled in the floor to drain out the waste. I got the opportunity to ride in the cockpit, which was really fun. So, planes went from scary to very interesting!" I thought for a moment as I envisioned that and said, "Well I'd have loved to ride in the cockpit, but not in the back!"

This isn't for the faint of heart, so reader discretion is advised! Here she goes, "Later that night, they told me they had a real treat for me. I was going to see a bloody plane! It was a 707 retired from passenger service, whose new job was to haul naked quarters of beef. The holes in the floor from where the seats were bolted down were now used to attach the nylon straps to hold down the quarters of beef. They'd stack it up to the level of the bottom of the windows! They also put it in the baggage holds, and when they opened that up . . . I can still remember the smell of it. It should have made me more afraid of planes, but instead I found it really interesting. It was the same exact kind of plane that I was in for the emergency landing—same exact kind of plane." I'm now envisioning her description of the crate full of frozen pig guts.

Temple is always seeking to learn more, and this was no different. "I also read a lot about planes and how they fly, and that also helped me to get over my fear of flying. Now, I sleep on planes. I sleep through take off, but not through landings, because that's a good way to wreck your ears."

120

Chapter 16

The topic of panic attacks was mentioned. "When I was afraid to fly for those three years, I'd have a panic attack on the way to the airport. But you know what? I did it. I simply did it! Today when I listen to people talk about having panic attacks, they shut down. I'd be having such a terrible panic attack that I'd be choking, but I did it. I'd get panic attacks having to face some of the feed yards, too. There were lots of things that gave me a panic attack, but I'd do them all. That's the difference in people today, they don't do it. The other day at an airport, I talked to a nineteen-year-old boy who had never shopped or taken public transportation. I said to his mom, 'This summer he's going to learn to shop and ride the bus.' This is ridiculous that these kids are being sheltered like this."

Temple is spot on with this statement, as always!

Here was another unpleasant flying experience. "Many years ago, I was on a Boeing 737 from Tasmania to Australia, and the turbulence was so violent it was like a giant dog had the plane in its mouth thrashing it around. They had announced ahead of time that it was going to be rough. We were flying over the Australian Bight, which is known for having rough air. It was the worst turbulence I've ever experienced."

Okay, I'll let you in on this little tidbit. Anything concerning bodily functions will instantly get Temple giggling and snorting like a little kid. It's highly contagious, and you won't be able to refrain from joining her. "Then, there's the world's worst vomit flights! This was about twenty years ago. We get twenty minutes into the flight, and a man stands up in the front of coach and starts barfing. But instead of using a bag, he starts walking towards the bathroom, barfing on everyone as he's walking along. He managed to get it on a third of the plane! (Temple is now giggling like a young schoolgirl, squealing in delight.) Fortunately, I was sitting far enough back that I didn't get hit." Now the sound effects came, with Temple imitating the sound of someone vomiting. "People started throwing their blankets on the floor to cover the vomit. I can remember the flight attendants trying to push the drink cart over the blankets, and seeing vomit all over the wheels."

"There was another flight I was on, flying out of Denver. We had just lifted off, when this girl leans over next to me and starts vomiting! I unbuckled my seatbelt and jumped out of my seat, as the flight attendant started yelling to sit down and buckle up. Fortunately, there were some empty seats two rows down that I quickly slipped into and put my seatbelt on. I looked, and there was vomit all over the seat I'd just been in. Instead of using the bag, that girl leaned over to puke on *me*!"

I'm having a laughing jag at the moment, but then came more: "Just recently, Teresa was on a flight, sitting next to this girl who vomited all over herself, and she just continued sitting there. The flight attendant came and told her to go to the bathroom and clean herself up."

Don't ever be sick on a plane if you're flying with Temple. Or at least don't aim at her!

CHAPTER 17
Getting in the Back Door at Colorado State University

I called Dr. Bernard Rollins, the professor that Temple contacted all those years ago to seek a teaching position at Colorado State University. He was one of the people that got up to speak at Temple's seventieth birthday celebration. I could hear that he was speaking from his heart as he talked about Temple, telling the huge crowd about that phone call he received many years ago from the young, persevering Dr. Temple Grandin.

"Dr. Rollins, thank you for taking the time to talk to me about Temple," I stated, "What do you recall from that day she first called you?" He replied, "I'm in a different field from Temple, so I can't talk about research we've done together. Here's what I remember about when I first met her. She already had her PhD, and was doing research and making a name for herself. She called me stating she wanted academic affiliation. I assumed that was for a number of reasons. One, of course, was for credibility. When you send in papers, you want it to say, 'Temple Grandin, Colorado State University.' The other thing she wanted was colleagues. She definitely wanted to be in agricultural cattle country, and it's a great town. It all seemed incredibly rational to me!"

Curious, I asked, "When did you figure out she has autism?"

"I think I knew that from the get-go, back in the seventies, but it didn't matter to me. I told her I didn't know if I could get her a job there. When I approached the department heads in vet medicine and animal science, I already knew of her reputation and all the positive changes she had made, so it wasn't that hard of a sell. She wasn't looking for a bunch of money. I think it's been great for the kids, and it's been great for the school. As far as having autism, everybody has things that are better and worse. Temple is terrific with the students. Remember at her birthday party when all her graduate students got up to sing her 'Happy Birthday?' Well, she's not married; these students are like her children, and she's like their mother, in a very good way, a very nurturing way." He continued, "Were you aware of the fact that she totally funded eighteen graduate students? Everything. They walk out the door with their PhD, totally debt-free."

I said, "Well, I just learned this at the party when Temple announced it. I was truly shocked." Dr. Rollins replied, "I know professors all over the world, and have never heard of anything like it."

He continued, "I've never once seen any sign of arrogance or having grandiose feelings. She's always the same. And she's gotten better with all her social skills. When she came over to hug me at that party, I was in tears. When I first met her, she wouldn't even shake hands. You know, there's nothing I'd want to change about Temple. I think the world of her. Her work is her life, and it's a very worthy life." I agreed wholeheartedly, "Indeed, it is."

Chapter 17

I enjoyed talking to Dr. Rollins, both to listen to his New York accent, but also listening to him talk about Temple. That was another pivotal point in Temple's career.

CHAPTER 18
Jim Uhl the Building Contractor— A Big Door Opens

I was extremely excited to have the opportunity to talk to Temple's good friend, Jim Uhl. Jim sought her out to help with a project after someone told him about her. Temple's career really took off once she became friends with Jim. They spent the next ten years together nearly every day, mostly with Jim and his crew, and often Jim's wife, too. Temple has had numerous long-term friendships and business partners over the years. Yes, this book is about Temple and all the stories she has shared with me, but the people whose interviews I've included in this book are the one's Temple has had a relationship with for many years, often twenty or more. That's pretty impressive for anyone, but even more so for someone on the autism spectrum. You learn a lot about Temple's character hearing these stories. The rest is history, as they say.

I started out the conversation by asking Jim how he first met Temple, where they met, and what his first impression of her was. Here's Jim's story about Temple, in his own words:

"First let me back up a little and tell you why I met her. I had a background in concrete and steel, and a long, long road of growing up in Arizona with cattle people. This was back in the seventies, and there was a big need in the cattle market for contractors to do specialized work for livestock handling and holding facilities. That just fascinated me, and I wanted to do it. I got to know a fella that had been the vice president of a large company and had specialized in these facilities. He and I became friends, and I told him that I was just starting out and only had one or two men with me. We can't do something that big, but we can certainly help the local people who had asked for smaller jobs. I said that I see the animal handling facilities, and I understand how to build them, but I don't know the exact dimensions and the designs. There was no such thing as an architect who designed these things, you just sort of built it. He then went on, 'Well you know, there's this young woman who graduated from Arizona State University in the livestock department who seems to have a great knowledge and fascination for this type of thing. She has a scientific mind and enjoys drawing, but may be difficult to meet. She may be reluctant to meet you, but I'll give you her name.'"

Jim continued, "So I got her name, and she had an apartment over by ASU. I called her, and finally got through to her. Temple is a very forceful person, and she has a lot of courage and great personal strength. She wasn't about to meet some guy that wanted to do this and that, and didn't want to be involved with somebody she didn't know. She was very, very hesitant. So, I don't know what I said or did, but I asked her to meet me right there near the university and have a sandwich or a cup of coffee and talk."

Chapter 18

"After a reluctant start, she agreed to meet me. I think at the time she was working down at the packing plant here, stunning cattle, the job of actually putting the cow down. So we did meet, and she came directly from the packing plant. That's a pretty rough job, as you can imagine, and her mode of dress (Jim started chuckling!) was pretty, uh, unusual. Particularly for a woman during those times." My curiosity got the best of me. I wanted to know what exactly Temple wore to that first meeting, so I asked him to describe her attire. I was grinning as he described it, "She was wearing boots and jeans, a long sleeve western shirt, and she had been working hard all day. You have that normal amount of manure and blood and sweat all over you—in your hair, your face, all over you! It comes with the territory, you can't do it any other way. Anybody would look like that. I don't want to be dramatic here, but it was a bit shocking to me. Well, maybe not shocking, but unusual. But we sat down, and I didn't act as if it made any difference to me, or that I even noticed, and we talked."

Jim went on, "For some reason, Temple and I hit it off. I assume Temple had you talk to me because she felt that same chemistry with me that I felt to her. That planted the seed of getting to know her. She invited me to come see how livestock work, why they do what they do, and why it was unnecessary to crowd them, punch them, or abuse them. I don't want to use that word, so I'll say 'treat them in a rugged manner.' You can instead treat them in a manner that appeals to them in their natural instinct. You can cause them to do what you wanted them to do, need them to do. Walk down a lane, stop, start, turn, don't panic, don't stampede, don't hurt each other or anybody else, and quietly and calmly go forward to accomplish the task you needed to get done. Rather than dragging them, beating them, pushing them, stinging them with shockers, and screaming at them, there was another way." This was very exciting for me, to listen to Jim tell the story. It was like a movie coming to life.

So, here comes the squeeze machine. Jim described, "She showed me the machine she had built, and," he laughed, "put me in the machine! By this time, I realized that there was more to Temple's scientific research than just trying to make a name for herself in cattle. There was a feeling in me that this was a greater calling, a higher calling. She was a very unusual woman. She was very bright, very aggressive, very forward, she said what she had to say. There was just something unusual about Temple. When she showed me the machine she built for herself that hugged her, I didn't know anything about autism. I had heard the word, but knew nothing of it. Over time, as she got to know me, she'd start saying things like 'a person with autism doesn't really want to be touched.' You don't necessarily go up to Temple every morning and hug her. But that doesn't mean she doesn't enjoy saying good morning to you. That machine sort of took the place of that."

Jim goes on to describe his thoughts on Temple being different. "I realized I was dealing with a very unusual person here, but I was fascinated, and became completely convinced that she knew what she was doing. In order to build something like this, it had to be done right. She agreed to provide the proper design, and I was just delighted! Temple is a good business woman. She reads *The Wall Street Journal* every day, I mean, she knows business. I didn't think money was the motivating factor, but money is a part of business. She wanted everything just right, and didn't want her name on it unless it was perfect. She showed us what to do: put that up, take this just down, repair this, fix that. We were simply delighted to do whatever she said to do."

"How did your men handle her?" I inquired.

"The men I had working with me were very unusual, and they took to her. Temple has leadership ability and they began to believe in her like I did. If she said, 'Take it down and put it up right, you did it all wrong,' they would do it. These were macho guys, I'll tell you that, but they took a liking to her and believed in her as I did, so we did things the way she wanted them done. And so that began the relationship that went on for at least ten years. My love became doing Temple's work. We did lots of other jobs, too. My company sometimes did fifty million dollars' worth of work a year. I liked doing the other work, steel structures and concrete structures for industrial purposes, but I loved doing Temple's jobs. The most fascinating thing was to work with Temple to build these livestock handling facilities that she designed. When we'd be building them, she'd come to the job site, and she wouldn't leave until the job was done!"

"Boy, you two sure spent a lot of time together," I commented.

"Yes, we did," he responded. "We'd have lunch and dinner together every day. We were together seven days a week, because we worked at least six, but mostly seven days a week. The facilities that we built would take the cattle from the range, to the feedlots, to the dipping vat, all the way there to the packing plant kill floor. I never did anything beyond the kill floor. Once the animal was stunned, there were great companies in the United States who had wonderful designs for handling the animal. I'm going to use the word 'stunned' instead of 'killed.'"

Jim was specific, "Nobody had any real designs prior to Temple. There were only one or two people that I'm aware of in the United States who had any kind of designs to do with the animals when they were alive. How do you handle them? A lot of that technology was known, but a lot was not. Even if it was done correctly, like down in Texas or up in South Dakota, Temple went to those locations and watched those operations work. Temple is a master photographer. She'd photograph them, then stand there and measure everything and draw them. She brought these designs from California to Texas, Arizona, Wyoming, New Mexico, and brought them together and consolidated them."

Temple got to meet the legendary actor John Wayne. Jim shared this, "Let me digress a moment, there was a man down at John Wayne's feed lot, Red River, which was a major feed lot in Arizona with nearly one hundred thousand heads of cattle. The guy who owned it was Ted Gilbert, a very prominent cattleman here, very forward thinker. He was raised in the Santa Barbara, California area in the twenties when there were big cattle ranches there, and spent his life in the cattle business. He was a very sophisticated guy who looked like he ought to be in Hollywood himself; he was handsome, sophisticated, refined, and flat knew cattle. He gave us a wonderful job at Red River building a dip vat, which gave me the opportunity to do bigger work in that industry than I had ever done before. I remember very well standing there with Ted one day, as we were watching Temple go out and inspect the work that our men were doing. He said, 'You know, I've spent a lifetime working with cattle, and I've dipped thousands and thousands of heads of cattle, but if you told me to tell you exactly how many inches apart this was supposed to be here, and what angle that was supposed to be there, and what degree turn that was supposed to be, I couldn't tell you! But Temple can tell you, because she's gone out and measured and documented what works, and cataloged that and indexed it. She's just terrific!'"

Jim continued, "Ted and his wife, Lillian, adopted Temple as their great friend. Until the day that Ted died, Temple was one of his favorite people, and Temple loved Ted and his wife."

Jim shared more about Temple and her work. "I didn't design anything. Temple designed everything, I only did what Temple told me to do. I believed in her then and I believe in her now. She was the designer, and we built according to her designs. She was also doing scientific writing and getting published. Temple works twelve hours a day, seven days a week. She's a human dynamo, in love with her subject. It'd be nothing for Temple and me to leave Phoenix together and drive to Reno. During these drives, I said very little and she talked about a wide variety of subjects. I found her fascinating. I had been privileged to be around some very intelligent people; I got to spend a summer with the

President of Harvard Medical School. Temple is very, very bright, so if you'd ask her about something, she would talk about it. I learned a lot from Temple, just absolutely fascinating!"

I thought this was really cool. Jim said, "I was in the Marines during Vietnam. As an example, I'll say that if you were going to be in a very difficult situation and you could pick someone to be with you, Temple would be the one I'd pick. Temple doesn't give up, she doesn't quit, and she isn't intimidated by anybody. The guys I had working for me, many of them were older than me. One was over twenty years older than me, and I loved him like a father. Well, he loved Temple, and he always called her 'Miss Temple.' The other guys (and myself!) treated her with respect, and they knew she was providing them with work. She also was nice to them, and she helped them. If one of them was lifting something heavy, Temple was right over there at the other end helping him lift it. If one of them got cut or hurt, she was also right there helping them. She'd clean it up, put a bandage on it, asking them, 'Are you okay? I'm going to watch you.' She's the real McCoy." That says volumes about Temple, right there.

How People Reacted to Temple

I asked Jim about how people reacted to her. He said, "I'll break it down into two categories, maybe three. There were some people who didn't know what to make of Temple. They had probably never been around anybody like that, with her type of laser- beam intelligence, her being vocal, or her being able to get up in front of a large group and stand up there and speak. She was aggressive, and wasn't afraid to walk right into wet manure and check something out. Those people were kind of shocked by it. Then there were others who just automatically knew that this was a person who was deeply committed to what she was doing, who had admirable qualities of courage, determination, and observation. She's an observer, communicator, and has a 'never say die' attitude. These could be people from all walks of life, from average to the very top echelons of business. It depended on their ability to accept her. There were cattleman and important business men who absolutely could not accept her, but they are idiots!"

He continued, "With a lot of the other cattlemen, if they misbe-haved, the other ones would pull them aside and reprimand them and tell them to act like a gentleman. I don't necessarily think it was gender-based. There were highly successful men and women in the cattle industry that just didn't want to hear what Temple had to say. There was one time I took Temple out to dinner, and this woman kept saying things to Temple to antagonize her. This woman wanted me to do her job. She kept going at Temple. Finally, Temple hit her fist on the table! I then told that woman to leave Temple alone, or I'd leave and let her pay the restaurant and do the building herself. I told her I was not going to jeopardize my relationship with Temple, because she wanted to show Temple she knew more than her. And she didn't! She immediately stopped, and everything calmed down. Some people sim-ply couldn't take Temple. They just didn't know what to make of her. It appeared that they were intimidated by her. I don't want to use the word 'unusual,' because I feel like I'm being disloyal to a great friend and a person I respect tremendously. They just simply flat out didn't know what to do with Temple, and they were sort of in shock. The rest of us were sort of in awe! Our family doctor here in the Scottsdale area was, until his death, an extremely well known, brilliant guy with a great personality. Temple was having a problem and didn't have a personal physician. She wasn't feeling well, so I told her I know a great doctor and I called him for her. She then went to see him. The next time I saw that doctor, he said, 'That young woman is highly unusual, and very brilliant.'"

I found Jim's description of all those people's reaction to Temple to be exceptionally interesting. As someone on the autism spectrum, throughout my life I've experienced exactly those same things with various people. Looking back, I realize they simply didn't know what to make of me or how to deal with me. My demeanor was pretty much the same as Jim's description of Temple at that time. But those who did like me thought I was the greatest thing since sliced bread. This is a phenomenon of being on the autism spectrum.

Jim was very insightful. He continued, "Then there are the people who see beyond the superficial differences, and recognize that this person has a huge amount to offer. Let's quietly listen and extract that information, because the overall goal of doing something well and correctly supersedes the various personality traits as long as we have a great end result. So what if Temple's personality or mannerisms were somewhat different?" Exactly. So what?

Chapter 18

I cringed at this story: "Temple did a lot of things that were highly dangerous in order to understand the behavior of livestock. I think her parents would have lost their breath if they saw the things she did to gain scientific knowledge that nobody else had. For instance, I don't know if you know how hot Phoenix can get, but on a load of cattle going to the McElhaney feed lot—which is about a two-and-a-half hour drive—she snuck inside the cattle hauling truck and recorded the temperatures and behavior of the cattle. Let me tell you, that was one dangerous move. If those cattle had shifted, they'd have crushed her. But afterward, she knew the heat stress that was occurring to those animals." When he mentioned the McElhaney feed lot, I asked him, "Did you know about Temple going up flying with Sam McElhaney in his Baron?" Jim got to laughing about that and shared, "Sam was a gentleman, like most men from back then, and I can still see Sam hobbling along with his cane to get to a fourteen-foot iron gate open for Temple and ushering her through. He absolutely loved her—when they liked her, they loved her! Just talking about Temple brings a lot of warm feelings to my heart."

I went on to tell him, "So, here's what Temple told me about flying with Sam. She said she got to fly in the cockpit of Sam McElheney's Baron, up to his feed yard in Wellton, Arizona when they were working on the dip vat. One time, when they were coming back, Sam flew right across the path of a jet as they came in for the final approach. The air traffic controllers started screaming at him, and he simply yelled back, 'Yeah, I saw it!' Sam always had his dog, Booger, flying in the plane, and there was dog hair everywhere. The first dip vat project was at McElheney's feed yard. By this time, Temple was totally over her airplane fear." Jim bellowed, "That's quite a story about her and Sam!"

I asked Jim if he knew Temple when she got thrown out of the Scottsdale feed yard. Laughing, Jim started, "I'm at Scottsdale feed yard right now! It's kind of funny you asked me that. Well, in the 1970s I did a lot of work for the Scottsdale feed yard, and I knew them well." Jim shared his thoughts on why Temple got thrown out of the Scottsdale feed yard that he asked not to be in print. He went on to say, "Temple could be in your face, and she could be aggressive. You know, she comes from a very fine family. Temple and I had what I call adventures and good eating!" He chuckled. "We worked hard all day, then I'd say, 'Why don't I take you and I out to dinner?' and we'd have a nice quiet dinner someplace. She loved it and I loved it too, and we'd get away from the crew and have a nice meal. Rarely was our work in Phoenix, so we were always on the road. Temple was very nice to my son and my wife, and she knew my mother. We looked out for her and her welfare, and tried to make these projects enjoyable. In recent years, she's told me they were the most enjoyable years of her life. I never permitted any one to treat her in any way other than appropriate for the occasion. If any of my men would have treated her in any other way, I'd have fired them!"

Reminiscing, Jim recalled, "One thing that stands out is the time when we were working at a job out in Fresno, California at the O'Neil Meat Company, and Muhammad Ali was going to fight Spinks. Temple knew about it, and she said, 'You know, Jim, every place we go you take me to nice places, and you do what I'd like to do, and you know it! I'm going to take you to dinner at a place where we can watch that boxing match on a wide screen TV.' So we did that together, and she sat there through that with me, and I thought that was really nice. I remember that forty years later, and bring it up to you because it was just courteous in that manner. I'm a huge Temple fan, and have absolutely nothing negative to say about her. Only positive things. I think she's wonderful, she's made a contribution to the livestock industry, and she helped me build my company."

I could sense that Jim was getting overwhelmed when he started saying, "But all along, I began to figure out that Temple was answering a greater call. Her study of animal behavior was assisting her in understanding the difficulties she had as a child, and was continuing to have, so that she could improve the lives of children, understand them, and help them to live a better life. And when I came to that conclusion, then forever and always, my heart is with Temple, because that's a higher calling."

"Jim, how did you feel when the movie *Temple Grandin* came out and she exploded into superstardom?" I asked. His response was, "None of the guys who are still alive, nor myself, were the least bit surprised. We thought this film was long overdue, as we all knew that we had a star in the making."

Nearly at the end of our great conversation, Jim volunteered, "I feel I knew Temple during the formative years about as well as a person could know another person intellectually, because she was so open. I can remember being at the San Francisco airport with her and the plane was delayed for many hours. So, during that time, Temple explained Einstein's Theory of Relativity to me!" He laughed quite heartily. "I can still remember sitting there being entertained as she explained it to me, with my jaw dropping."

Yep, that's Temple, helping you learn something new every day.

Follow Up with Temple After Jim Uhl Interview

After speaking with Jim Uhl, I talked to Temple to ask her about specific things from that conversation. I started out asking her about John Wayne.

Temple was excited with this conversation. "So, I hear you got to meet the legendary John Wayne! What was that like?" I asked. "At the time we built that dip vat, John Wayne owned Red River feed lot," she began. "He had also owned 26 Bar Ranch, and I got to see him at the bull sale. He gave me a ranch catalog that he signed, which I gave away to somebody. He was just a big cowboy. He looked exactly like he did in the movies, he even dressed the same! He died not too long after I saw him. At the time I did the project, he owned the feed yard. I knew what a big movie star he was, and it was exciting to meet him. He was a rancher guy, really tall. I don't get awestruck the way some people do. When I was in

Chapter 18

high school, my roommate was swooning over Ringo Starr on the floor in front of the TV, watching him live on *The Ed Sullivan Show*. Girls were ripping out the grass that Ringo Starr walked on, and I'm going, 'Really?'"

I said, "When I was talking to Jim, he mentioned a guy named Ted Gilbert." Temple replied, "Yes, Ted Gilbert! He was the manager at Red River feed yard—a great guy, a fantastic guy. See, the feed yard got sold. There were very big death taxes, and they had to sell the ranch and feed yard to pay the death taxes. Ted and his wife were great people. Great friends."

Temple went on to talk about the dip vat job, "The McElhaney feed yard where we did the first dip vat was about three hours away. Red River was only an hour away. So, while they were building it, I was there the whole time, making sure they were building it right. I could just drive there every day."

"Temple, Jim told me about the time you treated him to dinner to see the boxing match," I said. Temple surely remembered, "I can remember once when we were in Fresno, the hotel only had little tiny TV's. Jim loved boxing, and there was a big match between Ali and Spinks. I wanted him to get to see it on a big screen, so I took him out to dinner. That job was where I spent an entire day handling all their cattle, and was having some trouble with the cattle, then I realized it was my shadow! The cattle could see my own shadow! So then I had to position myself so they couldn't."

People Who were Bad, and Good, to Temple

I then brought up the Scottsdale feed yard, and the day Temple got thrown out. I was kind of worried about how upset she'd get over it.

I started, "Temple, Jim and I talked about the day you got thrown out of the Scottsdale feed yard." Temple quickly stated, "When I got thrown out of the Scottsdale feed yard, it was the foreman that did that. The owner of the place was actually very nice to me, but he wasn't there very often. It was always the foreman that gave me all the problems. I just found out about five years ago from someone who knew him that he was a big 'macho' guy. He used to belong to some big club in Scottsdale that was for men only. He just didn't believe that women belonged there. I didn't understand that back then. Remember, that was back in the early seventies. I can remember when I was driving into the Scottsdale feed yard, on the radio was playing that song by Sonny and Cher, 'A Cowboy's Work is Never Done.' Temple started singing the lyrics here, in a nice tune: "I used to jump my horse and ride, I had a six gun at my side, I was so handsome, women cried, and I got shot but never died! That's what was playing that day I got thrown out! At that time, the only jobs women did at the feed yards were in the office. So, right after getting thrown out, I drove straight to the *Arizona Farmer Ranchman* magazine office and offered to write a column for them, called 'The Feed Lot Bulletin.' I had already written several articles for them, and I wanted to go to the Arizona Cattle Feeders meeting to cover it for the magazine. Boy, did I write the best article ever; I got everything correct, and everyone's name right. It was in a fancy Arizona hotel. My revenge against Scottsdale feed yard was to get that press pass and write really good articles, then they'd have to let me in."

As Temple was recalling those fateful days, she thought of this, "I started thinking back of all the people who were good to me and I realized many of them were ex-military officers, like Jim, who was a Marine Corps captain. Military people appreciate logical thinking. Jim Uhl was somebody very critical in helping me get started."

I asked Temple, "Jim Uhl said you called welding 'pigeon doo-doo,' and he said he'd let expand on that for me. What was that all about?" Temple replied, "That was before I met Jim. I criticized someone's welding and said it looked like 'pigeon doo-doo,' and Harvey Winkelman (the engineer at the plant) called me into his office. He explained to me that the welder, Whitey, was his employee, and that I should have come to him if I didn't like the welding. He explained that Whitey was a maintenance engineer, which was different from a construction engineer. And even though Whitey's welding wasn't pretty, they held. He sent me into the cafeteria where Whitey was to apologize for my rude talk. He told me exactly what I had to do. He counseled me very well. He didn't scream and yell at me. He just talked to me in private that my behavior was not acceptable. I just went into that cafeteria and did it. Today I was reading an article about adversity, and how kids that have a certain amount of adversity that rise above it often accomplish more in life. There were some of these things I just had to learn from my mistakes."

"Yes," I said, "but a lot has to do with how you get counseled. When someone yells at you or is in a mocking way, it's meaningless. When it's done right, it will enable you to learn from the experience."

CHAPTER 19
Temple's Life at Home

Try and envision Temple's home. What do you conjure up in your mind for the home of a world-famous person who's a jet-setting phenomenon? Possibly you are thinking of the show *Lifestyles of the Rich and Famous*. Far from it. As I have come to know Temple extremely well, I've learned that things like a big fancy home aren't on her list of things to have. While I was in Fort Collins for Temple's seventieth birthday bash, there was no time to go visit Temple's home. I did get commentary from two people closest to her, Cheryl Miller, her long-time assistant, and her friend and business partner, Mark. I asked each of them to describe Temple's digs. Their response was pretty much exactly what I had guessed!

Cheryl shared this, "Temple owns a small two-bedroom condo. One of the bedrooms is her office, and it has lots of file cabinets heaped with papers. She has a stack of publications near her small copy machine that contains articles she has written. Her living room has tons of mementos from meetings—beautiful awards, a handwritten note from Claire Danes that is just lovely, and a small leather horse, also from Claire Danes. Her windowsill is filled with little cows, sheep, etc., that I am certain people have given her. She has a wonderful old picture of her family property near the front door, pictures I have framed for her of her awards, her brain scan, posters, etc. She also has paintings people have done of her and lots of hand-painted cow pictures. Of course, there are awards and trophies scattered all around, as well."

"Her TV cabinet is filled with favorite books, and those that people have signed and given her in appreciation for writing blurbs for their publications."

"Her kitchen is her second office, with her computer in it. She has a huge box of fan mail from the HBO movie *Temple Grandin*. She is saving those because they mean a lot to her. She does not cook at all in her kitchen; in her refrigerator you would probably just find yogurt with fruit in it. Her kitchen counters are tidy and have baskets and such of nuts and chocolates that have been given to her."

"Her basement has metal shelves, I think three or four, that I had my son build for her because she had so many boxes of books in her living room. It also holds her journal publications and other miscellaneous papers."

"She owns a small house on several acres that has a stream running through it. Her design assistant, Mark, lives there, and he owns some horses and maybe cows. I asked her one time why she doesn't live there, and she said she prefers, and feels safer, having people around her. They actually kind of watch out for her. Her condo is about a mile from my house, so it makes email exchanges very easy. Yes, Temple's place is very modest." I enjoyed hearing Cheryl's commentary on Temple's style of living.

Chapter 19

I asked Temple if she cooks much when she's at home. Her reply was, "Well, no, I have yogurt and fruit in the refrigerator, that's about it. I have a big lunch out, then either just some snacks or take-out for dinner." I asked if she drinks coffee. "Yes, I do like coffee. There's one thing I do hate, and that's pumpkin spice coffee!" I took this one step farther, "So, do you make your own coffee at home?" Sighing, Temple confessed, "No, I have to go out to get it." I started wondering if I should get her a coffee machine that uses the little cartridges. Probably not. I'm guessing it would be sitting in its box years later.

Temple continued on this topic, "The problem is that I'm just gone so much! When I am home I'm trying to catch up on correspondence, writing papers, reviewing articles, or reading my scientific journals. I recently got an email from a mom who had contacted me ten years ago about her son. I had told her to get him out working. She wrote to tell me she followed my advice, and now he's married and has a good job, and she wanted to thank me for talking to her back then. I've now got her email hanging up on the wall. I figure I'm doing well. Maybe if I was home more often, I'd do more stuff around here. I'd probably have a dog. I really like Labrador retrievers, so that's what I'd get. It would be fun to take it to the office with me."

Temple was on a roll, "I just want to see these young kids be successful. They're not learning any working skills. I've been running into moms who can't let go. Part of the problem is that their identity is tied up in being a special needs mom. See, Mother's sense of identity was tied up in her theater, where she did semi-professional theater and music, and some TV shows. She had her identity with that, and it had nothing to do with autism. In fact, I can remember when I was a kid, I didn't like the fact that she spent so much time at the poet's theater. It made me want to tear up the tickets and stuff. What they should have told me was that I liked having my life flying kites and making things, and Mother likes to have her life with her theater friends. I think if they would have explained it to me that way, I would have accepted it a lot better. It should have been explained to me that I have a life, and then I would have understood: I liked to fly kites, I liked to build things, I liked to find shells on the beach and make stuff out of them. That was my fun stuff to do, and Mother had her fun stuff to do."

Parents, take note of that. Don't ever underestimate your child's feelings or thoughts. Explain things to them. They might not look like they get it, but they really do—they're just not showing it on the surface.

Teenage Years at Home

When Temple was a teenager at home, before going to boarding school, she had her times of great emotion just like any other teenager. Here's one that I would have loved to be a fly on the wall for.

Temple mentioned that she once kicked a hole in the wall when she was angry. Whoa! Let's get the scoop on that! "Mother made me fix it. I had to paint the entire section of the wall so it didn't show." "Gosh!" I exclaimed, "Why did you kick a hole in the wall?" Temple continued, "I got into an argument with Mother, and I got so mad I kicked a hole

Chapter 19

in the wall. I had to buy all the materials to fix it; I had to get all the spackling and tape. It was a small enough hole that I didn't have to cut out a piece of drywall. I stuffed it full of newspaper then put the tape over it, then the spackling. I had to do a really big area and feather it all out, then come back two days later when it was all dry and sand it until it was totally smooth. Then, I had to paint an eight-foot by eight-foot area of wall to be sure it all matched. I'd seen other people do all that, so I knew how to do it. I got all the tools and just did it. Mother had said it better not show, and it didn't. It looked perfect. I never kicked a wall ever again!"

"Where did you learn to do drywall work?" I asked. "I once saw people doing it, and I stood and watched very carefully and saw what to do. I simply memorized it, taking snapshots in my mind, and stored for future use." Amazing.

CHAPTER 20
On the Job

I'll admit to eating meat. Then, I'll admit I'm an animal lover. I guess I pretend that those packages of New York strip steaks, or the pork roast, or the organic chicken tenders I buy each week were magically made in a factory. I'm thinking that not too many people stand there while making their selection and imagine just how all that animal protein got there in the display case. Since meeting Temple, that's exactly what I do as I stand there. And here's how I justify buying meat. I will bet you any sum of money that if Anita Lesko stops buying meat, the meat industry is not going to go out of business. So, the next issue is how the animals are treated and processed (yes, the word "processed" is the pretty word for "slaughtered"). This is where Temple Grandin gallops into the picture on her white stallion!

Before she came onto the scene of the meat industry, it was the norm for animals to be inhumanely treated and slaughtered. Temple dramatically changed that, not only in the United States, but around the world. When I recently asked Temple about the number of facilities she's designed, she said, "It's not the number of facilities I've designed, but the number of cattle processed in plants I've designed. Well over half of all cattle in the US are processed at facilities designed by me."

I said, "They should put a little sticker on meat packages that were produced at your facilities. Then I'd feel better about buying it." If you take the time to investigate the difference in how animals are handled and treated at a non-Temple facility vs. a Temple facility, you will find it's like night and day. Temple has done amazing things for the autism world, and she's done equally amazing things for animal welfare.

I want to be sure you see something else about Temple: that she does, in fact, have great compassion for animals. In one of our last conversations for this book, Temple brought it up on her own. I was really happy she did, so I could share it with you. Temple started, "I've been bashed by animal rights activists because I design slaughter plants, but on the other hand, I've been bashed by the meat industry for things that I've stood up for. It's like equal opportunity bashing!" Hearing this, I replied, "Yes, I can imagine how that could happen." She continued, "Somebody wrote online that I didn't care at all about the animals. I got to thinking, 'Now, wait a minute! I've gotten into a lot of trouble for speaking out concerning issues with the cattle.' The animal activists that have criticized me don't realize that I've faced backlash by people in the livestock industry, too, because I've spoken up when there's been a problem. We've just got to speak out on this stuff."

I replied, "Oh, I know that when people bring bad things into the light, others don't like it. But otherwise, it would all still be happening. This process needs to be done humanely. And that's what you are all about."

Chapter 20

Temple went on, "The animal rights people don't like that I'm trying to fix slaughterhouses, not get rid of them. One of the really interesting things is working with the restaurant companies. You get those vice presidents out in the field, and they see something done poorly, and they instigate true undercover boss moments. They say, 'Oh, we've got some things here that we are going to have to fix!'"

Temple added, "Right now heat stress in cattle is a big issue, it's becoming more and more of a problem, and I'm the one who's bringing it up. A lot of people don't want to know about it. It costs a lot of money to construct shade." I replied, "I remember talking to Jim Uhl about the time you snuck into the semi-truck loaded with cattle on a scorching day, so you could monitor the heat level and stress on the cattle." She replied, "These big, heavy cattle need shade in their feed yards, and that costs money. Someone has to stand up and say it when there's something that needs to be fixed. I just read a paper published in the *International Biological Meteorology Journal*—it's not my paper, but I quote it all the time. It's about open-mouth breathing in cattle, and it discusses that the more they pant, the hotter they are getting inside. They only pant when they're really hot and in trouble."

I asked, "How can you determine how hot they are getting?" Temple explained, "When they're at rest, cattle breathe with their mouths closed. When their mouth starts opening, they're getting hotter, and the more their tongue extends, the hotter they are getting inside. This especially happens with high humidity, high temperatures, and no air movement." You had better remember this for the next time you are at a feed lot in the summer!

Temple can get really deep, and I remember there's a genius on the other end of the conversation. Temple was on a roll about the meat industry, and said, "The other thing I started thinking about is the ethics of eating meat. I just read the other day that there was an experiment done—you know how DNA has four base pairs? (Of course, I'm sure this fact is right on the top of your head.) This experiment added two additional pairs to make six base pairs. You're talking about being able to make life from scratch."

Of course, there's more. "I thought about that back when I had to write an ethics paper back in the late seventies. I knew that diabetics got their insulin from cattle, from their pancreas, which would give them a ten-day supply. That made me feel pretty good about slaughter. That changed when human insulin was made from bacteria. That was the first Genetically Modified Organism (GMO), but it wasn't called that back then. GMOs hadn't been invented yet; back then it was called r-DNA, or recombinant DNA. It was a new form of life to replace the steer pancreas that was used to produce insulin. I got to thinking, then, that maybe in the future, we were going to create more forms of life. That's an ethical issue that makes slaughter houses look like a walk in the park."

"Now they're talking about growing 'meat' in the lab where they get the heme molecule, so it would be juicy like a steak, but use soybeans. But they're going to have to modify the soybeans. No matter what you do, you'll be making a new form of life. In the future, we are going to be able to create any form of life we want. If we want to make dinosaurs, we can create them. This is going to create huge ethical issues. There won't be a need for slaughter houses anymore." This is Temple the scientist at work, even when she was just starting out in her career. Her mind is never at rest, always thinking, always reading scientific journals, always analyzing ways to do new things.

Back to those cattle! Temple said, "We also have got to give these cattle a life worth living. We've just got to do that. We can't have them getting so hot that they're getting heat stress, or rough-handling them. Fortunately, that's been improved. Handling has gotten a lot better, that's the good news."

"Temple, how do those big E. coli outbreaks occur in the meat industry?" I asked. Her answer isn't for the faint of heart, I was sort of sorry I asked. Temple got very matter-of-fact and logical and told me, "It's very interesting in a slaughterhouse. It took our industry twenty years to determine the critical control point on how not to contaminate the carcass when you dress out the beef. We've known for as long as I've been in the industry that when you gut the animal, you have to hold the knife a special way so that you don't cut the guts. The thing that took them a long time to figure out was how to properly remove the skin off the back legs so that as you skin it, the hide falls away from the meat. Now, when you go into a plant and go to that area where that's being done, you can see that it's done with surgical precision. They found that is a critical control point for not contaminating the meat. There's a person that skins each leg out. One person skins one leg, another person skins the other leg. As they're skinning it, they have to be very careful to keep folding the hair side back on itself. They have a big steam device that they put on the leg after they take the hide off of it for sanitation purposes. That's one of the most critical points for not getting E. coli on the meat. I really like the that approach." I was picturing all this going on. Those New York strip steaks were becoming less appealing by the second.

Temple continued, "If you tour the entire plant, you can see those critical points. Another thing we've known for years is called 'tying the bung off and dropping it,' where they cut around the rectum and tie it off. They've done this for years, but the leg-skinning process they had to figure out. The front legs are taken care of by a hide puller, which pulls the hide down. At a big plant there's a thousand people per shift that work there. The plant can only do two shifts, and the third shift is clean up." I was thinking to myself that sometimes the operating room looks like a slaughterhouse after some big bloody trauma case. There will be blood all over the floor, chunks of flesh, bloody footprints out the door and down the hall. That environment isn't for the faint of heart, either.

"To make it absolutely sterile is impossible," Temple stated. "If you go into a cold room in a meat plant where they are cutting the meat, it's clean, but it's chaos compared to the area where they are doing the surgical precision work. The meat is tested daily, where they take samples and send it out to be analyzed. That's done as another safety measure. If they had the testing facility right there, you'd have people walking in and out contaminating everything. The results come back on the computer from the off-site testing facility."

"There's some smell on the slaughter floor because you're taking apart a warm animal. In the cold room, it doesn't smell," Temple added. I was starting to feel a bit woozy at this point. Becoming a vegetarian was starting to look very attractive.

The Great Trip to Australia

"I just came back from Australia," Temple continued. "I was on a really nice ranch where they had Herford and Angus cross cattle, and we went out to the feed lots and spent a day there. I gave cattle-handling talks and autism talks. Then we went to another ranch, over in Queensland. Australia is one of my favorite places because of the beautiful countryside and luxurious pastures. There, they call them a 'property' instead of a 'ranch.' I was petting a big Brahma, who was one of the 'coachers.' These coachers are tame cattle that are used to calm down the new arrivals. When you get new cattle in that's super wild, they put the coacher cattle in there with them, and that helps to calm them down. I got to see a lot of the countryside, which I really enjoyed. There are great pastures, and people are really getting into good cattle handling." I stated, "That's pretty interesting about the coacher cattle!"

Of course, this would have attracted Temple big time: "They have a really great program there called SUN PORK, where they're teaching people on the autism spectrum stockmanship positions with the pigs. Since they have introduced it, it has been very successful. There's no interviews required to participate. They start out at a 'pig fair' at a conference room in a hotel, where they come in dressed for the job in their coveralls. They do things like practice giving vaccinations by injecting oranges and ear-tagging cardboard pig heads, so that the equipment is not so novel."

Temple was having fun describing this whole thing to me. "By the time they actually get out to a pig farm, they've already used all the equipment and practiced, so they are ready to start for real. So when they are then handling a squealing, wiggling little pig, they already know how to handle all the needles and equipment. They're finding about 70 percent of the students are taking to it! It gets these kids who are addicted to video games out doing something. I'm not being an old fogey (I got a kick out of Temple using the term old fogey), but what I'm finding when I go out to talk to people is that these kids have two paths they go down: get jobs before they get out of high school and do well, or get addicted to video games and you can't pry them out of the house. That's what I'm seeing. The parents absolutely shouldn't be letting them do this. I tell the parents to limit the video games to one hour a day. Period. Give them choices of other things they can do, but don't let them stay holed up in their bedroom on the computer all day. There was this boy who was addicted to video games, but he wanted to do the pig program. In Australia they call pig farms 'piggeries!' So he went to try it, and had a massive panic attack."

Chapter 20

"I thought the idea of having the 'pig fair' in a conference room at a hotel was a really good idea," Temple stated, "and they even have to wear the specified clothes for the entire day with rubber boots. What that does is reduces the 'surprise factor.' If there was a problem, like the uniform itching, that can be taken care of that ahead of time. One thing I suggested to them was that because they use brand new uniforms, they wash them before wearing it. If I don't wash new clothes first, I break out."

Temple continued, "It all makes it less novel that the clothes they had on and the tools they use (like for tagging the pigs ear), are all familiar. Punching the hole through the cardboard is the same feeling as punching the hole on a real pig ear; the cardboard has the same resistance that a pig's ear would have. They make the oranges cute by putting little eyes and ears on them, and the students learned to vaccinate the oranges. There was water in the vaccine bottle, and they had to draw the vaccine out. The point was to get them to learn how to use the needles so that nothing was a surprise. You couldn't just have someone go out to a pig farm and get a squealing little pig, and then try and figure out how to use the equipment afterward. They already learn it in the conference room. There's also record-keeping materials and computers at the pig fair to show everyone, and tons of videos they must watch as part of the experience. The videos show people working with the actual pigs and using all the same tools. After they complete the training, they are taken to an actual pig farm and they try it for real."

I got quite the education on pig farms, or should I say, piggeries. It's actually pretty involved. "They also have to learn how to teach the piglets how to operate the automatic feeders. These feeders are triggered by the tag the pig has on its ear. You know how you have that card at a hotel that's used as a key, that you hold it over the sensor on the door and the door opens? These feeders operate the same way. The pig must be taught how to walk through the gate, and then the feed comes out. You have to be very gentle with these pigs. Most farms realize that they need someone to be their 'pig whisperer' to train the young pigs. When the pig learns to open the door, they go inside the feeder and their ration comes out. If that pig gets scared during the learning process, they won't go inside the feeder. It takes a very special person to do this, one with a lot of patience."

Temple is all about encouraging young people to try lots of things to find out what they like. She said, "I've talked to five students who tried the pig farm training. Four of them loved it and one hated it. But it's really important to find out what you like or don't like."

Did Temple Ever Get Hurt on The Job?

I asked, "Temple, have you ever gotten hurt on the job?" Not surprisingly she answered, "Yes, very early in my career I did. At a feed yard in Texas, a gate smashed in my face and I busted my nose! I didn't want anybody to know about it, so I went and looked in a mirror and straightened it, then went right back to the feed yard. I never let anybody know that I was hurt. That was the only time I got hurt around the cattle. I'm super careful when I'm around the cattle! The other injury was from falling on the stairs from the office; I fell flat on my back and really hurt myself. Once, I slipped and fell at a restaurant and hit my nose on the corner of a table and busted it a second time." "Where was that?" I inquired.

"It was in a restaurant right in Fort Collins, Colorado, the week before my trip to Germany," she explained, "and the next day I had to talk to a room full of executives from McDonald's. When I woke up that morning, the day after my fall, I had a big black and blue eye, and my nose looked horrible! I quickly found a store that sold makeup and bought some foundation. I went back to my hotel room and did a great cover up with that makeup—by the time I got done, you couldn't see the black and blue area. That was the last time I wore cowboy boots!" I was right next to Temple the third time she busted her nose. I'll share that story later on; it happened right at Colorado State University, on her seventieth birthday. I nearly fainted.

Temple Created Her Own Internships

Back to Temple's job. "Temple, how did you get into all those feed yards in the 1970s?" I asked. "First, I'd go there and just say I was a student and would like to observe. I'd spend around twenty minutes just observing. Then, I'd just step forward and do something; they'd usually let me do it. But I'd watch for a good long time first. Then they'd get to know me, and they'd let me run the chute and bring the cattle up. There was a certain amount of assertiveness necessary! Just act like you're supposed to be there. In addition to working at all these feed yards with the cattle, I went over to the Swift Plant, and they got to know me, so every Tuesday afternoon I'd go over there. My reaction was to go out and do stuff. You can fight anxiety by getting out there, or staying holed up in your room. When I started going out to those feed yards and working with the cattle, my anxiety went away." I commented, "You were pretty brazen to pull off that whole thing at one feed yard after another!" Proudly, Temple replied, "Yes, I was indeed!"

As is typical with highly successful people, Temple stated, "I've always had a goal. Like when I went up to the editor, just like the movie shows, and asked him for his card. Then I wrote an article based on my master's thesis about head gates for cattle chutes. When I got kicked out of Scottsdale feed yard, I thought, 'I'll show Scottsdale feed yard, I'll start writing columns and get a press pass, then they'll have to let me back in.' That was my goal! Scottsdale feed yard was something that had to be conquered. At that point, I was getting really interested in the design of cattle facilities. That press pass could get me into national meetings."

Remembering something from her childhood days, Temple shared this, "I'm trying to look at the assertiveness trait that we both seemed to have." She was referring to me. "I can remember a trip we took to Canada; there was a toboggan slide. Nobody in my family wanted to go on the toboggan, so I couldn't rent one, but I talked another family into letting me ride on theirs. I was about ten or eleven at the time of that trip. I simply asked them if I could ride with them, they let me, and

Chapter 20

I had a blast! That took a good amount of assertiveness to do. When I started painting signs at the Arizona State carnival, I just went up to an old sign painter and showed them some signs I painted, and he put me to work. Next thing I knew, I was painting signs all over the carnival. That then evolved to the cattle handing facility, but it's the same sort of thing. I enjoyed seeing my signs in front of people's exhibits."

Temple had a few more tidbits about jobs, "The oil industry is an open door to get in, get a job, and work your way up—as long as you can read at the sixth or seventh grade level. At a meat packing plant, you can learn every job and work your way up to foreman, but you're going to have to learn fifteen different jobs."

A thought sprung to my head suddenly and I exclaimed, "Oh yeah, I'm reading a biography about Elon Musk!" Temple replied, "He learned how to work at a really early age. That's the only way to do it. Did you read yet about some of the awful jobs he had when he was young?"

"I haven't gotten that far yet," I replied.

Temple's Favorite Quotes

Ok, if you're still with me here and haven't fainted from visions of the meat industry, I want to share some of Temple's favorite quotes that she shared with me.

"Obstacles are those terrible things you see when you take your eyes off the goal," Temple told me once again. "In the seventies, I saw that on the wall of the art building at Arizona State University. That's by Henry Ford. At that time, I didn't know it was written by Henry Ford,

and back then I had no way of looking that up. It was on the art building wall. Then I had a plant superintendent tell me I had to persevere,
and a cattle buyer at the Swift plant tell me that 'trouble is only opportunity in work clothes.' That's a quote by Henry J. Kaiser."

Here's another one of Temple's quotes, "Abstractification—I wrote
about that in *Animals in Translation*. Here's what it is: you know, you
look at some philosophical writings that are so abstract you just can't
understand it. It's like someone making policy for healthcare and
they're so far removed from the field that it's becoming so abstract it
doesn't even apply. See, policy makers need to avoid abstractification!
That's one of my little made up words."

"Another good one is 'illegal, but not bad.' Yeah, there might be
some things that are against the rules, but not really bad. Like things
you have to do to get your construction projects done."

I really like this quote. "Here's another, similar one, '"The trouble
with opportunity is that it always comes disguised as hard work.' It's
anonymous."

Here's one that Temple just loves! "'Heat softens steel. Then, I can
bend it into pretty grillwork.' This is about how change takes place on
animal welfare. When a video comes out with something really bad, the
industry gets all excited, and gives you the opportunity to change it. This
is how change takes place with a bad practice. Then, I'll explain that we
want to make pretty grillwork and not have a mess. That the steel is soft
when it gets heated, and the change you make is a constructive change.
You don't want to vaporize the steel. That won't accomplish anything."

CHAPTER 21
Temple's Friend Mark

I t may come as a big surprise to many, but Temple has a friend that she's known for over twenty years. They go to lunch and dinner together, movie night out, or simply just hang out together. Mark told me that he has a few other acquaintances, but he'd rather spend his time with Temple. "Temple loves to read and keep up with the news and current world events. There's always something to talk about with her, something really interesting," Mark told me.

I asked Temple how she met Mark, and it was quite a story, not surprisingly! "He came to me. He had a theory about horse hair whorls. He'd observed that horses who had the hair whorls on their forehead were flighty. He was a horse-shoer, and had observed this when he was shoeing lots of different horses. He had already tried to talk to people at other universities, and they just sort of ran him off. I listened to him, and said, 'Let's do an experiment!' We did it with cattle. We used fifteen hundred cattle, and looked to see if there was any correlation of having a hair whorl on their forehead to how much they jumped around in the squeeze chute. We found that there was! In fact, I was the only one who would listen to his theories about it. So, that's how we met each other originally; he came to talk to me at my office at Colorado

State University. We did that study twenty years ago. After that, we did other scientific studies together. Then, I sent him to computer school to learn Computer Aided Design (CAD) drafting. He started doing all the drawings for me of the animal handing facilities and equipment."

Mark described what he does at Colorado State University. "I help Temple with her lab at the farm, I teach the kids how to draw, and help them with their homework. Temple splits the class (the undergraduate students), and half go with me and half go with her. Then at the half-way mark, they rotate. That's been the routine with her lab for twenty years now. I designed that facility."

Mark continued, "When we did that study about the hair whorls, we discovered that the higher the whorl—and it's the same for horses and cattle—the higher their nervous system reactivity. That reactivity controls how keen their senses are. That increased sensitivity to the environment predisposes them to being fearful. Those 'flighty' traits also correspond to intelligence. If you raise them correctly they can turn out to be the very best horses, but if you raise them incorrectly, people call them crazy and stupid because they're slow to learn due to being preoccupied with fear. All this research brought Temple and I together, and that was back in 1993. We did research for about five years, and then she taught me to draw and design facilities, and I've worked for her company (Grandin Livestock Handling Systems, Inc.) ever since. I do a lot of design work, and I do a lot of international work in China, Mexico, and South America for her company as an animal welfare consultant. A big job I just did in Mexico had multiple feed yards, and

Chapter 21

I helped them understand what it was going to take to get a European import license. They wanted to sell their beef to the Europeans, but the Europeans have animal welfare guidelines that you have to meet to export into Europe. These are the kind of things that I do."

He went on to share more, "Temple has been far more than a boss, she's been the best friend I could have ever had. As far as friends go, she's the kind of friend I've always wanted. I have a few other friends, but I really don't like to hang around with them and talk about football or stuff like that. I'd rather spend my time with Temple talking about serious things like our work, or current events. Temple can really let her hair down around me, whereas around many others she's so politically correct and careful in her words. I admire her not only because of all she's done for animal welfare, but how she is as a friend, and how she takes care of those who are close to her: friends, students, and mentors. She shows that she really cares. People with autism are not known to be like that. I've wondered about that for years. I think her friendship comes about from routine and experience, and the more she calls you, the more experience she gets, the bigger the photo album in her mind. The more information she stores about you from tying it to experience, the more intimate she can appear." I thought this was an extremely important concept that Mark put very nicely into words. I see it apply to all ASD individuals building friendships and relationships from routine and experience. It also shows the need for patience with this population. Mark went on, "Where now, Temple's not 'on the spectrum' to me. Temple is just Temple. Everybody has their own idiosyncrasies, and Temple's are just a little bit different than other people's. Temple is so straightforward and honest. She's the kind of friend anybody would like to have, and she's there for you if you need her. I can tell you a funny anecdote, without going too personal. I was in the hospital once. So, you know, when something happens to a friend, and you call them to see how they're doing, they might say, 'Oh, I'm fine.' Well, you know they're not, because they were just in a horrible accident. So then you say, 'Oh come on, man, I know you're not doing well, it can't be easy, so if you want to talk about it, I'm here.'"

"With Temple, if you say, 'Oh, I'm fine,' she'll say, 'Okay,' then go on to the next subject. She takes it literally! Once you understand this, you can accept it. Now, if I were to have been honest right away and responded, 'Oh, I'm in a lot of pain, and they gave me some new medicine that makes me feel horrible,' she'd go into problem-solving mode! She'd go on for the next hour, problem-solving the situation. She doesn't quite understand that you might just want to talk and vent your feelings regarding your accident." Yes, ASD individuals can and do take things literally. That's why being honest and straightforward with us is crucial. We can't read faces or guess what you really mean.

Mark shared another event, "All those years ago when we first met, I had never, ever been around slaughter plants. So, the first time I went out, I saw a bloody mess. This was in the mid-1990s, before audit by large buyers forced the industry to improve. It was horrible; I came away from that with a mild case of Post-Traumatic

Chapter 21

Stress Disorder (PTSD), and I couldn't understand it. For a few days afterwards, I was feeling pretty down. I was having dreams about it, and all the classic symptoms of PTSD. It was Temple who recognized that in me and asked me, 'What the hell is wrong with you?' So I told her, 'It was that whole experience at the slaughter house. That's just so wrong!' She then asked me, 'Well, what would you do differently?' I said, 'I'd just let them all go!'"

Laughing, Mark proceeded, "And then she said, 'Mark, you're a pretty smart guy, but that's the stupidest thing you've ever said! Just think of what would happen if you let them all go. They'd be better off in that slaughter plant than running all around starving to death, getting chased by dogs, or getting hit by cars!' She was right. Then, she asked me what else I thought was wrong with the slaughter plant. Well it seemed to me, that after they shoot the cattle, they have a reflex where they kick. When they pull them up on the rail, they're still kicking. I figure it's them venting their anger at just getting killed! So I had gone way, way off the emotional deep end. Little by little, Temple used her logic to talk me out of the irrational fear that was underlying my post-traumatic stress. She said, 'Mark, the cattle were calm going up into the center track restrainer. You've seen them struggle in a feed yard just for vaccinations.' And I thought, as a matter of fact, that's right. I've seen cattle getting vaccinations and becoming stressed out, but they were calm at the slaughter plant. What got me so upset there was the volume of animals, over two-thousand a day! That's two hundred and forty in an hour! I was up on the restrainer all day, I mean, I was covered with brain splatter and blood, and it was the most horrific experience. I think I'd have gone off the deep end if Temple didn't grab me by the hair and pull me back up to the surface. I went on to learn a lot about what goes into these processes; I became an expert on death to overcome my fear of being around it. I look at it all differently now: like changing the oil in your car, without an emotion to it." Mark had a lot more courage than I, as I'd have fainted the minute I saw all that taking place!

Mark learned everything from Temple, obviously. "When I go down to a big slaughter plant in Mexico, I'm very responsive to the level of fear in the animals and the people. Twenty years after Mark's first experience in a slaughter plant, he visited several plants in Mexico and was horrified to learn that the employees on the kill floor, and the managers, believed that reflex kicking was a sign that cattle were still alive, and they were skinning live animals. Nobody had told the employees that brain-dead cattle can have kicking reflexes for five minutes. This lack of understanding was prevalent and the psychological effects on the employees was probably devastating.

"In the time before they are going to die, it's our moral and ethical obligation to make sure they're not fearful. When the people balk at that concept, I then tell them there's an economic benefit and there's meat quality issues that are involved in killing low-stress animals. You make more money if you treat them better. That goes all the way from the slaughter plant back to the home ranch. The happier they are, the healthier they are, and the healthier they are, the better they grow, the less likely they are to get sick and need antibiotics or vet care, and all the labor involved in treating sick animals. There's a lot of economic advantages to it, and that's a really good selling point. These are the issues Temple and I focus on the most. Many people can't focus on the ethical aspect, because to them it's just stupid animals and it doesn't matter. However, the economic aspects do matter to them. That's the magic of Temple, the logic of her: she sees the big picture."

So, would you like to meet me at a steakhouse for dinner tonight? At least I order my steak super well done—absolutely no pink.

CHAPTER 22
The 9/11 Disaster

I bet every person can remember exactly where they were and what they were doing on the morning of September 11, 2001. It is something that I still am affected by, and thought I'd ask Temple about it.

I started out, "Temple, let's talk about the 9/11 disaster. Where were you on that day?" Temple stated, "On 9/11, I was at home. It was a Tuesday. I was at my desk, and Mark called, exclaiming, 'Go turn on the TV! A plane just crashed into the World Trade Tower!' So, I jumped up to go put the TV on, and just as I did, I saw the second plane crashing into the second tower, live. I said 'Oh my God, that's a jetliner!' One side of me was horrified, the other side of me, the engineering side, was impressed that the building held when the plane crashed into it. Then I had to go to my class, but it was just a short class. The towers collapsed during it. Once out from that, I was wondering why those buildings collapsed. They absolutely should not have come down."

Those on the autism spectrum can easily get obsessed with something, myself included. Temple was heading in that direction. Here she goes, "I then started playing every video I could find of it, over and over again, trying to figure out why it collapsed. One side of me was just horrified about it, about all those people dying, but my engineering side wanted to find out why it happened. I knew that something was wrong with the design of that building, so I started watching all the channels to see pieces they were picking up out of the rubble pile. I saw they were picking up beams with plates on the end of them with bolt holes in them. I saw that none of the plates were deformed. What that tells me is that the fasteners sheared off. *The New York Times* never printed a diagram of the building, but about two weeks later, the *Chicago Tribune* printed a drawing of how the building was built. When I looked at that I thought, 'You've got to be kidding.' I can tell you exactly why it collapsed: there was no vertical concrete in it. They took trusses, like you'd have in the ceiling of a supermarket, and put a thin concrete slab on them to make the floors. When that type of truss gets hot it becomes a wet noodle, and so it just yanked the fasteners out on the side. I also think there weren't enough fasteners."

I thought I had read everything about that disaster, but I never saw this. She went on, "Two years later, Massachusetts Institute of Technology (MIT) came out with a study showing there weren't enough fasteners, and they all just pulled out. Those concrete slabs just started coming down and pancaked. They should never have collapsed. If they had been built like the Sears Tower, they never would have collapsed. No one will ever build a building with that design again. They had designed those towers for ease of fabrication, and cheap cost. If there had just been a fire in one of those buildings and the sprinklers had failed, it would have come down. That shows a lack of visual thinking. See, when I looked at the trusses, I immediately envisioned a supermarket

Chapter 22

when it's burned down. The roof is collapsed because as soon as the trusses get hot, they bend. That building was strong like a cardboard box, but when you wet cardboard, it's all soft. When the trusses started sagging, the concrete slab literally slipped down and smashed onto the floor below it. When I saw all the plates and none of the holes were deformed, it told me that the bolts sheared off. A mathematical mind doesn't see these things. There's a difference between cheap and safe, or that which kills a whole bunch of people. There's a difference in how unethical it is."

"I know you were up in the World Trade Towers when you went to the Windows on the World restaurant. Have you been to the World Trade Towers 9/11 museum?" I inquired. Temple replied, "No, I've never been there." I continued, "I was there a few years ago. It's pretty emotional. I was there with my husband. We both felt the presence of all those souls that died that day in the museum, especially when we were in the lower level where the steel beams are housed; the section where the plane flew into. It took us days to recover from being there."

CHAPTER 23
Recent Trips

Between our talks, Temple continued to make her frequent trips all over to speak, either for autism or animal handling. She had just returned from Ireland, where she visited two beef plants.

"Hi, Temple. How was your trip to Ireland?" I anxiously inquired. I heard papers shuffling around in the background as Temple replied, "At one of the plants, the cattle wouldn't go in the stun box. You know how we fixed it? Turned out there were six holes, about an inch in diameter, that had been drilled in the gate, and the cattle could see movement through them. We covered them up with tape and then it worked just fine. I still get a thrill out of figuring these simple things out."

"I know that you really enjoy figuring stuff out, simple or complex," I added.

"What did you do at the other beef plant you went to?" I asked. She replied, "I showed the other beef plant I went to that they were bringing too many cattle up at once and letting them turn around. I showed them how to only bring up a certain amount of cattle and keep them moving along going forward. Then it worked just fine. This was just a small plant, only processing thirty-five cattle an hour. The big plants process around three hundred and fifty an hour. But I really like figuring out how to fix things, especially something simple like that."

"I don't think I've asked you this question yet, but where have you traveled around the world?" Temple thought for a moment, then began firing off the list of where she's been. It was quite an impressive list. Here's what she had to say: "I've been to Australia, New Zealand, the Philippines, Japan, Thailand, China, Hong Kong, England, Scotland, Ireland, Denmark, Norway, Finland, France, Italy, Switzerland, Bulgaria, Chile, Argentina, Uruguay, Brazil, El Salvador, Costa Rica, everywhere in the United States, Canada, and Mexico. My favorite place is Australia, because they have lush pastures and I love the countryside."

"What was the most unusual thing you experienced while traveling abroad?" I wanted to know. I was sorry I asked after I heard the answer. "At a dinner in China, they served big sea slugs. Nobody ate them, they looked like big, slimy dog poo! There was no way I was going to bite into that. You'd have to just pick it up with some chopsticks and just pop it into your mouth! I can also remember going to a meat science meeting in Finland, and the meat was terrible!"

I think I'd be looking for a restaurant nearby.

CHAPTER 24
Looking Through the Lens

I'm sure you've seen those beautiful photos of Temple sitting with cattle, the ones with her black shirt and red scarf, and endless others. Have you ever wondered who took those great shots? Well, you're going to find out! The photographer is one of Temple's great friends, Rosalie Winard.

"Temple," I asked, "how did you first meet Rosalie?" Temple replied, "Years ago at an autism meeting, she was doing a documentary on a man with autism who was nonverbal. That's where I first met her. I've been over to her house a whole bunch of times. She's really into photography. She had a beautiful art exhibit on bird photography. Rosalie has taken a lot of photos of me, like those photos of me in the red shirt with all the cattle. She's taken some of the best pictures of me. She took the pictures of me and Oliver Sacks, like the one with our arms around each other in his office. I needed to have pictures taken of me, so I had her do it. It sort of evolved from there."

I asked how long Temple has known her. "Oh, about thirty years!" she replied. "That's a long time to be friends with someone," I observed, "I think because you are friends with her, you were relaxed in front of the camera, and that shows in all those photos."

"Oh, you'll like this story," Temple shared, "Rosalie had this cat named Earl Grey. He was a big, blue-point Siamese cat. He was a tool-using cat. He would wad up a towel, or shirts, and hump them!" She burst out laughing. "I'm not kidding!"

By now, I was laughing too. "I've never heard of a cat doing that! Good grief! Was he neutered?" I asked. Temple replied, "I think he was neutered late. If they get neutered late, they keep some of that behavior."

Temple continued, "When I was a kid, we had a Siamese cat, and he was neutered late. He'd see his reflection in a framed picture that was leaning against the hall wall. We had just moved in, so things weren't hung up yet. So when he saw his reflection in the glass, he'd back up to it and spray it. He must have done twenty pictures, and it went under the glass in some of them!"

"Oh, that must have smelled great," I added.

"Rosalie told me that sometimes she'd come to visit with you and travel together," I said. Temple replied, "Yes, Rosalie has traveled with me, yes, we've gone places together. She'd come to New York and we'd go to dinner with Oliver Sacks together, several times, and that was really nice. That's when she took those photos of me with Oliver. I'm really glad to have those photos. Rosalie and I also went to see *Avatar* together. That's such a wonderful movie."

I went on to say, "When I was talking to Rosalie, I mentioned that I went to your seventieth birthday celebration. She said when she went to see you the next day, you were packing your nose. She said your nose was broken and you were tending to it. That's what I was afraid of," I stated.

Okay, let me fill you in on what happened the day of Temple's party. She and I were heading out of the Animal Sciences building, on our way to the parking lot to go to the farm. We were walking pretty quickly. The front entrance of that building is basically a wall of glass, from the ceiling to the floor, with doors that are glass, too. I was looking straight ahead, walking next to Temple. All of a sudden, wham! Temple had walked right into the glass wall, full speed, and smashed her face into the glass. She bounced backwards, and I reached out to catch her, thinking she was going to fall. I actually heard a loud crack, which turned out to be her nose as it hit the glass. I went into a silent panic. I thought in that instant that she'd suffer a concussion from that impact. "Oh my God! Are you okay?" I blurted out. Without missing a beat, Temple replied, "I'm fine. I'm fine. Don't worry about it." I was worried about it, though, because I knew how hard she smashed into the glass. We then continued to walk to the parking lot and were soon on our way to the farm. Every little bit I'd ask, "Are you sure you're alright?" I kept watching her closely for any signs of a concussion. What else would a medical professional do?

Later that evening at the party, Teresa Corey asked me if I noticed the big bruise on Temple's face by her nose. I said, "Oh, I'll tell you what happened! We were walking out the front of the building earlier today, and she crashed into the glass!" I was motioning towards the front entrance wall of glass. Teresa continued, "Oh, dear! Was she okay?" I said, "I kept asking her the rest of the afternoon, plus I was watching her for any signs of a concussion."

"Temple, when Rosalie was telling me about your nose, I told her what happened." Temple replied, "Walking into the glass was the stupidest thing. I wanted to see how these boat winches lifted up the roof of the tent. They assembled the roof of that tent on the ground, then cranked it up on the poles with a bunch of boat winches. I was intent on seeing how that worked. I've seen those tents before and I wanted to know how they got the roof up there, so I wasn't paying attention where I was going." I reassured her, "Well, it's very easy to do because the glass goes from the ceiling to the floor, and it's crystal clear. The next day Rosalie saw you, she said it was really bad." Temple was her logical self, "I got some makeup and covered it all. I had to put some on the other side of my face and feather it out and make it look balanced." I asked if it was still painful the next day. She replied, "Oh, no. Only when it first happened. That's the third time I've broken my nose." Hopefully, it's the last time!

Temple shared, "Rosalie does some really great photography, and she has a book out called *Wild Birds of the American Wetlands*." I said, "Rosalie told me about that book and all her extensive travels to capture those beautiful images." Temple added, "Did Rosalie tell you that she has a national traveling exhibition of that book, and huge photos?" "Yes, she did," I responded.

Chapter 24

I'm very happy that Temple has so many long-time friends, like Rosalie. They've been friends for over thirty years. That's pretty impressive for anyone, but all the more for someone with autism.

■ CHAPTER 25 ■
Temple's Graduate Students
"In Their Own Words"

During my visit to Fort Collins, I had the extreme pleasure of meeting Temple's current group of graduate students. At Temple's seventieth birthday celebration, I also got to meet a few of her former students, who were already out in the work force with great careers in the meat industry.

Temple told me to meet her at the Animal Sciences building at ten thirty in the morning to sit in on the class she would be teaching at that time. I left the hotel in plenty of time to get there, walked across the street, and was already on the campus of Colorado State University. The weather was beautiful, a cool fifty-six degrees, with a clear sky and warm sunshine on my shoulders. The evening before at dinner, Temple had given me explicit directions for my journey, of course, written on a napkin. She was sure to draw the specific landmarks I should look for as I went along. Sure enough, I found each one easily, and went on looking for the next. That walk took me back in time to my younger days on campus at the various universities I attended. There were thousands of students walking along the pathways: some alone, some in groups, some on bicycles, and some on skateboards. Flowers were everywhere, beautifully landscaped, and views of the

Rocky Mountains peaked between buildings. I was savoring every moment, knowing that the day would unfold with one exciting event after another.

Finally, I spotted the Animal Science building. I just stopped for a few moments to look at it, knowing that inside was one of the most famous people in the entire world. Rays of sun were peeking through the tall, majestic pine trees that flattered the building's façade. Directly in front of the building was the "quad," which consisted of the most thick, luxurious grass I'd ever seen, and trees dotted at the perimeter. There were workers scattered everywhere, busily assembling the huge tent which would later house Temple's birthday bash. I checked my phone to see the time, both to be sure I was on time for Temple, and to see how many hours the workers had to complete their task. I was ahead of time, as I typically am for everything, but I wondered how the big tent would be up in time for the party.

I proceeded up the steps and into the building. I'd never seen anything quite like it before. I was used to being in buildings such as hospitals and operating rooms. This housed offices and classrooms for students going into animal sciences and the meat industry. There were large photos of cattle, pigs, and chickens on the walls, and hoof prints painted on the floor. There were chairs with cow hide, fur included, as the upholstery. There were big screens with videos playing, flickering glimpses of Temple. Staff were walking around, some with cowboy boots, some with muck boots, and some with cowboy hats. I was correct in my assumption that if I asked anyone where to find Temple, they

Chapter 25

would know. A woman directed me downstairs to Temple's office, but when I didn't find Temple in it, I called her. She said she was up on the second floor in the glass room overlooking the quad. So up I went, and found Temple in the room with her students. Temple had them all introduce themselves after she introduced me to them. They had just completed their class, so it was perfect timing.

Temple wanted all of us to go to lunch together, so off we all went: myself, Temple, and the six graduate students. As we all walked along, I made a little project of watching the faces of the oncoming students who saw Temple. It was obvious that the majority recognized her, but she wasn't aware of them looking at her. When we all got in line to order our lunch, I got exactly what Temple ordered, which was two kinds of meat, vegetables, and some hummus. The students picked up the tab for Temple and me. We all then made our way over to a table in the huge dining area. I observed Temple interacting with her students as I talked with them. Temple loves to keep up on world news, and had picked up a newspaper on the way into the building. She opened it up, briefly scanning the front page for anything to share with us. There were no lulls in the conversation. Temple loves to talk, and was sitting there with her students who share her passion for the animal sciences. Ample conversation, laughter, and eating continued for the next half hour.

I got to talk to the students during the walk over to the dining building, during the meal, and then later at the farm when Temple took me out there after lunch. That experience, seeing Temple working with the cattle, was a real highlight. I got to see her as well as her students herding the cattle through the cattle squeeze chute, then releasing them one-by-one. I was right there in the thick of it, getting to see it all before my very eyes. It was very surreal, like the *Temple Grandin* movie coming to life, only this was the real thing! I had to pinch myself to be sure I was really there. I was taking in every detail: the smells, the sound of the cattle walking, everything.

The farm, owned by Colorado State University, was about twenty minutes away. I got to ride with Temple in her vehicle, which I thought was yet another highlight of the day. How many people get to cruise around town with Temple Grandin at the wheel? She was a great driver, following all the rules of the road just like I do. I savored each moment, even when I simply walked with Temple from the Animal Sciences building to her vehicle.

I will share this, as I feel it to be amusing; I admit to having the inside of my vehicle exactly like Temple's! Here I thought I was the only one whose front passenger's floor area had books, magazines, and journals all over it. When I opened the door to get in and saw it all, I asked her if she'd like me to pick them up and put in the back seat. She shook her head and said "No, you can just step on them. Don't worry about it." She's my kind of friend! Without missing a beat, I climbed in, scanning everything on the floor and smiling to myself. It was all scientific journals, cattle magazines, and some autism publications, too. I thought it was grand. I hooked up my seatbelt and glanced over at Temple. She buckled in, then reached over and put on the radio to a news station. She stated she wanted to catch up on the latest events. I didn't know if it was alright for me to talk while she drove, as I didn't want to distract her, so I remained relatively quiet. My mind, however, was racing. It was extremely surreal to me, being in that SUV with Temple. She simply seemed bigger than life. I've been in her presence before, so that was nothing new, but for whatever reason it was a really big deal to me. The thought crossed my mind of taking a photo of her at the wheel, then I thought she'd think that was too cheesy. I took the photos in my mind, which I'll always remember and treasure forever.

I know this book is all about the stories that Temple has shared with me about her life. After meeting her students and hearing their stories of how their lives were changed by Temple, I decided that you need to hear these stories, too. I'm sure many people wonder if Temple continues to teach, how her students like her, and what exactly is going on regarding her academic career. Well, wonder no more! I asked each of them to write something I could include in this book for everyone to see Temple as a university professor. It was very apparent that Temple's students love her, and they clearly indicated that she greatly impacted their lives. Many of their responses brought tears to my eyes. Following are their stories, in their own words.

Kurt Vogel, PhD graduated from Temple's program about six years ago. I met him at Temple's birthday celebration. He's strikingly tall, and he instantly reminded me of the famous singer, Nick Lachey. I asked Temple about her memories of Kurt, and here's what she had to say:

"Kurt was a really hard worker. He got a lot done. He was very hands-on, and he was one of the few students I've had who could build all kinds of things. He had been working at a meat packing plant up in Wisconsin. He was just a really hard worker, he was like me, just got in there and got things done. He was good with animals, but he was really good at getting things done. He's a super nice person, always looking to see who he could help." Temple hadn't seen Kurt in years, and when she saw him, she threw her arms around him and gave him a big, squeeze-machine hug! She was quite beside herself to see him. It was a huge display of her feelings for him, and was very striking. I was happy to have shared in that moment.

Following are Kurt's own words:

Kurt D. Vogel, PhD

Associate Professor- Animal Welfare and Behavior

Department of Animal and Food Science

University of Wisconsin–River Falls

I met Temple in 2005 through an introduction by Jerry Karczewski, a long-time friend of Temple's who was the new general manager at Cargill Regional Beef in Milwaukee, WI at the time. I was in my under-grad at the University of Wisconsin–Madison, and worked at that plant during the summers and whenever I had time available during the school year. At the time that Jerry arrived in Milwaukee, I was working in the cattle procurement office and spending a lot of time in the barn

Chapter 25

helping to handle cattle, train handlers, and troubleshoot facility is-sues. I learned who Temple was in my animal science classes, but never expected to meet her face-to-face. I hoped to get the chance to attend one of her many presentations at some point in my career.

Jerry told Temple about me when he met with her at a conference. He called me to his office after he returned from the conference. I was about twenty years old at the time and I can still remember how ner-vous I was as I walked to his office, because up to that point in my life, being called to the boss' office meant that I had done something wrong. Jerry sat down at the conference table in his large office with me and said he had a friend who could offer some guidance on some of the facility troubleshooting I was doing in the plant. Then he handed me a copy of Temple's DVD, titled *Cattle Handling for Meat Plants*. Her business card was taped to the front and her home phone number was circled. My life changed when Jerry said, "She really wants to talk to you." That business card is in the frame on my office wall with my PhD diploma. It is a reminder for me of how one moment can change the course of your life.

The first time I called Temple, we talked for at least forty-five min-utes. I didn't realize that she and I shared many common interests until that phone call. That was the beginning of one of the most substantial and impactful professional relationships I have had. Temple was a part of my master's committee at Wisconsin, and invited me to work on my PhD under her mentorship at Colorado State University. In 2008, My wife, Laura, and I moved to Colorado so I could work with Temple.

Without Laura's support and Temple's mentorship, I wouldn't be where I am today.

The Cargill plant, where I met Temple and learned about cattle welfare at slaughter, closed in 2014. While I was working there, they gave me a supervisor-level hard hat with my name on it to wear. I keep it on a shelf in my office—it's another reminder of the events that have shaped my life. Temple came to visit me at the University of Wisconsin–River Falls, where I work now as a livestock behavior and welfare professor, after the plant closed. We were standing in my office when she looked up and saw the hard hat sitting on my shelf. Her eyes welled with tears and she said, "That was your doorway." Temple uses doorways as an analogy for taking advantage of opportunities and transitions in life. I completely agree. That plant was one of my doorways. I never imagined who would be on the other side of that door when I started!

Dana Wagner is one of Temple's current graduate students, who I met while at Colorado State University.

Dana R. Wagner, MS

Graduate Research Assistant

Animal Welfare Judging Coach

Livestock Welfare and Behavior

Department of Animal Science

Colorado State University

Chapter 25

Dr. Grandin has made a vast impact on me as a student, researcher, and person. While there are a multitude of ways she has positively changed my life, I will try to explain the most significant. When I was a sophomore pursuing my undergraduate degree, I thought I wanted to be a veterinarian. But I was having a hard time reconciling the dissonance of animal care on an individual basis versus animal care on a large scale. I had some mentorship through that period that helped to shape my ideology, but I remained teetering on the brink of uncertainty. By some luck, Dr. Grandin was coming to speak for a meat sciences class I was taking. Her talk was aimed at animal welfare in slaughter plants, and she was emphatically waving her arms about proper handling and that we need to "knock prods out of people's hands!"

She continued, passion burning brightly, speaking about proper handling and animal emotions. This was the first time I had heard someone in academia clearly stating things about animals that made intrinsic sense to me, but that no one had been willing to state outright. Animal welfare was a big picture focus, to use her words, and one that I immediately took to. I remember thinking, "Yes! This what I want to do," and first the first time in a year, feeling that my path forward was clear. That was the first time I met Dr. Grandin.

The second time I met Dr. Grandin, I was picking her up from the airport. I was finishing up my master's degree. Unbeknownst to me, her plane had been delayed on the runway, meaning that she was going to be twenty to thirty minutes late for pick up. I had looped around the airport about a dozen times, with panic beginning to rise in my throat that I had somehow missed Dr. Grandin. How one would lose one of the most important and influential figures in the world is beyond me, and I was certain I was going to go down in history as the student that lost Dr. Grandin, never able to show my face in animal science again. Alas, I had her phone number, and she answered on the first ring when I called to inquire where she was. She briskly stated the plane had be delayed when being taxied and that she was walking out. "I'm wearing a bright pink and red shirt with black cows on it," she said. I was barely coherent, still numb that I had her phone number. I finally found her, tucked her safely in my car, and drove back to campus with relief spreading across my chest. During the drive she asked about my project and my future plans. I told her about my research and that I wanted to pursue a PhD. She first told me that my research was, "important, and needs to be published." I remember feeling like a helium balloon had be filled in my diaphragm; Dr. Grandin said my welfare research was important! She then told me she had an opening for a student and that I should apply for the following semester. Me? Study under Temple? I had been secretly dreaming of such an offer since I had first learned of her and her work. Long story short, she offered me a PhD position later that night. I accepted it: a choice that has had a massive impact on my professional development.

Now that I work closely with Dr. Grandin, I've lost count of the number of interactions I've had with her. But a few things remain constant. I have never lost the wonder or inspiration in talking with her that I had the first time I heard her speak in person. Every meeting, every phone call, every weekly lunch, she inspires me to be a better re-searcher; she never fails to have an insightful comment on my research project. I have never lost the support she showed me in our second encounter; she told me my work was important then, and she still be-lieves in me to conduct and produce important work. Dr. Grandin can be direct, but the core of her motivation is to help one improve. She has shown me more support and kindness as a mentor than many, and one of her key qualities is her ability to understand without judgment. I will always try to emulate this with my future students.

Dr. Grandin is more than my major professor. I consider her a friend and mother figure; she cares deeply about her students and how they impact the world. She has invested time and effort in my develop-ment, both as a student and a person, and I can never fully repay her. I know I have the skills needed to help animals across the world, and even beyond that, she has helped me see how I can also help people around the world. I will always honor her grand legacy by doing my best to help animals, mentor students, and give back to my community. Dr. Grandin, thank you. Without you, many of us would remain in the dark, uncertain and confused. You have cast a great light on the world.

Miriam is one of Temple's current graduate students I had the pleasure of meeting, as well.

Miriam S. Martin

Livestock Behavior and Welfare

Department of Animal Sciences

Colorado State University

I grew up on a farm with all kinds of different animals and always knew that I would pursue a career that was tied to animal science. I went to college and I struggled with finding what I wanted to do with my life. I liked nutrition, reproduction, and meat science, but none of those subjects were my passion. I called Temple the summer before I graduated on a whim, and she encouraged me to come be a part of her livestock behavior and welfare department.

Taking her up on that offer is one of the best decisions that I have ever made. I finally found my purpose, and where I can contribute to the field of animal science. Behavior and welfare are tough subjects, our job is to find answers to ethical questions that lots of people in animal science are afraid to touch. Temple has been doing hard things all her life. Breaking into a male dominated industry—full of those who had no reason to listen to her thoughts, much less put those ideas into practice—was a tough mountain to climb. Temple is persistent. At seventy years-old, she still travels constantly because she wants to help people.

Chapter 25

Temple has no boundaries. There's no audience she is afraid to talk to, no issue she is willing to ignore. I've learned so many things from Temple. She has no affinity for earthly possessions, money means nothing to Temple. She funds our stipends and research in the behavior and welfare department through her personal finances. That is unheard of, but meaningful research that improves the lives of animals is what is close to Temple's heart.

Temple isn't afraid to get her hands dirty. At well over retirement age it would be easy to step down, and say it's time for the young folks to take over. Yet Temple still climbs up the walkway along the handling facility she designed out at the school farm, and shows students how to calmly handle cattle. She is as invested as ever in teaching the next generation the importance of animal welfare.

Temple reads scientific publications in the evening, and will come to school the next day with her eyes twinkling, wanting to share the newest break-through in science. She has a love for not only teaching, but also learning. She understands the value of cross-disciplinary research and working with people from diverse backgrounds to make impactful discoveries. Temple has taught me the value of being a lifelong learner with an open mind.

Temple has very distinct principles that she lives by, and that mindset translates to how she approaches animal welfare. She believes in doing things right the first time. Getting the opportunity to learn from her has changed the way that I see the world. I will always be grateful for the time I have gotten to spend with her.

I go to church with a little boy who has autism, and I think I interact with him better now that I know Temple and have a better grasp of autism. My mother works with ASD children, so I had some understanding of autism before meeting Temple. It sounds silly, but watching the *Temple Grandin* movie helped me better understand Temple, and many people have mentioned to me that the movie really opened their eyes.

Autism is part of Temple and her identity, but at the end of the day she doesn't let it define her. I think her willingness to embrace the challenges that come with it, but at the same time never play the victim, is really admirable. In some ways, watching how she approaches autism has helped us as her students understand how to work with her.

Truthfully, I just see Temple as Temple 99 percent of the time; her having autism doesn't even cross my mind when I'm talking to her. She's a very talented person with a unique perspective. It takes time to get to know anyone we come into contact with, and learn how to best interact with them. Getting to know Temple and work with her is no different in that respect.

I met Ruth at Temple's birthday celebration. She earned her PhD just a few years ago under Temple's program. Temple gave Ruth a huge hug, too. I asked Temple what stands out in her mind about Ruth, and here was her response: "Ruth was another person who was really good at teaching, a great teacher. She's now working for a company that audits food safety and animal welfare." I got to talk a bit to Ruth at the party,

Chapter 25

and she shared with me about when she was a student at CSU with Temple. She stated she was a single parent with a little boy, and that it is not easy working on your PhD with all that, but Temple helped her in many ways, and she's forever grateful for that. She remembered the time that Temple gave her little boy a great big hug. It meant the world to her.

Here's what Ruth shared:

Ruth Woiwode

Manager of Livestock Audit Services

Food Safety Net Services Certification & Audit

There have been so many moments of laughter and even tears with Temple that when I look back and reflect, it's hard to pick one that has had more impact than another—they have all collectively changed my life.

A memory from graduate school that stands out (of which there are many) was when Temple was giving the general seminar for the Department of Animal Sciences at CSU, and she was asked if she still uses her hug machine. Temple stated that it had broken some time previously, and said, "Now I rely on people like my friend, Ruth, for hugs." Initially, I was very embarrassed, because I was painfully shy and she had singled me out in front of the entire department. It wasn't long before I realized the impact of what she had said. I was her graduate student, but she had called me her friend ... probably the highest compliment she could have paid me. That message was driven home this week, while we were together. She kindly gave me a copy of her recent book, *Temple Grandin's Guide to Working with Farm Animals*. I asked her if she would autograph it, and she wrote: "To Ruth: a great friend."

Temple shared this with me about Erika: "She did animal welfare for McDonald's, then she went on as an independent consultant. I call her my non-matriculated student because she never went to the university with me, but we did lots of training out in the field. Now she's gotten to be a real expert on kosher slaughter, and I helped her out on that, too."

Travels with Temple

By **Erika L. Voogd**

President, Voogd Consulting, Inc.

I've always told myself that someday I would write a book with this title, but at this moment, it is someone else's that I am contributing to. I only have one truly famous friend, and that would be Temple. Eustacia Cutler did the world a big favor by naming her first born "Temple", as there are few individuals who possess similar talents, achievements, or accomplishments. By having such an uncommon and rarely utilized name, Temple herself became as recognizable as Oprah, Cher, and Sinatra! Of course, the embroidered cowboy shirt that has become her trademark also helps!

The first time I heard the name "Temple" was at the University of Illinois, circa 1979, when a friend of mine, Amy, was helping her with

Chapter 25

pig studies at the South Farms campus. Amy would tell me she needed to go work with Temple on projects and research. Temple also came to speak to one of my graduate classes on experimental design. She was already memorable, due to the monotone voice and subjects she shared about animal behavior and welfare. At the time, confinement and feedlot growing of livestock was taking off: more, bigger, better and faster. My classmates and I looked at her, knowing she was different, but I do not believe that at that time that I understood what autism was, or that Temple was considered to have it.

Years later, my work took me to Australia to visit a meat plant. Marie, my Aussie co-worker, bragged to me that the plant was a "Temple Grandin" design, and that Temple herself had crawled up the cattle chutes before approving the facility. Again, her name immediately identified who she was. Only a few months later, I was celebrating my fortieth birthday in Sedona, Arizona and saw Dr. Grandin featured on a documentary about calming livestock, including horses. I told my husband, "Hey, I went to college with that woman!"

In 1999, my boss handed me a proposal stating that the McDonald's Meat Safety Team was planning to add Humane Handling Auditing to the harvest plant reviews for beef and pork. The information explained that auditors would measure stun results, slips, falls, vocalizations (moos), and transport. I was doubtful about the concept of counting moos, but after visiting the first plant to train with Temple, I was fully on board. Humane handling became a passion, thanks to the contagious nature of Temple's enthusiasm and skill for teaching the

McDonald's System how to assess the stress level of animals at the time of harvest. During the early days, we were neophytes in our knowledge, so we called Dr. Grandin frequently to ask questions and verify results. She wholeheartedly and without hesitation returned every call, as she still does today, and shared her expertise at all hours of the day or night, regardless of where she was or where in the world we were.

One memorable measure of Temple's fame was the latest update on how often she was recognized in an airport. When I first met her, it was once in six trips to an airport. A few years later, one in four. Then, by 2003, one in two visits. Now, it is probably once on every street corner thanks to the 2010 HBO movie, *Time* magazine, and most recently, her induction into the 2017 Women's Hall of Fame.

I'm sorry to momentarily interrupt Erika's submission on Temple. She just mentioned about Temple's fame, and airports. Just the other day, Temple shared with me about the time she met Sigorney Weaver at London's Heathrow International Airport. Very excitedly, Temple said, "Oh yes! Well, I ran into Sigorney Weaver in customs at London Heathrow International Airport. She got me in the super elite line, and I went right through customs rather than having to wait forty-five minutes!" She thought that was pretty exciting. Obviously, Sigorney Weaver thought the same thing about meeting Temple Grandin!

Back to Erika's submission:

The interesting guidance that Temple has always aspired to, during her life and many accomplishments, is "never forget where you

Chapter 25

started and who you are." She still takes the same amount of time for a high-level CEO as she does for a parent in a third-world country who has a question about their ASD child. She has never failed to return my phone calls, regardless of the topic or level of urgency. We have traveled together to Hong Kong, China, Canada, Brazil and Australia. It is not unusual to find us singing childhood commercials while we drive. She has "wowed" foreigners with her "Oakey from Muskogee" lyrics, or the words to the *Bonanza* TV show theme.

I've got to interrupt Erika's piece once again. I couldn't resist this one! I remembered asking Temple if she has a favorite song or listens to music. Temple's reply surprised me! "I love The Phantom of the Opera! *I like to blast that out! I just gave a talk in a theater the other day that had an old Wurlitzer organ. I said, 'I wish we could play* The Phantom of the Opera *on that. I'd like to have heard that organ blow that theater away!' They said they don't play it because it would bother some of the kids with autism. I kind of felt upset that I didn't get to hear that old mighty Wurlitzer play!" What was surprising to me is I love that song too, blasting loud. There's nothing else I want to hear loud, just* The Phantom of The Opera.

It gets even better. Temple continued, sharing this tidbit with me. "One concert I was at, I remember I was at Arizona State University in a big hall, and they had a Virgil Fox heavy organ! Man, did I get into that! I stood up in the middle of the crowd yelling, 'Encore, encore!' as I was jumping up and down. They did a whole encore just because of me.

And I play Phantom *really loud in my car. Of course, I saw* Phantom *on Broadway, and it was wonderful. Michael Crawford and Sara Brightman were absolutely wonderful."*

Now, where was Mick Jackson when we needed him to capture Temple on film doing that?

Back to Erika's piece:

I have attended an autism seminar sponsored by Future Horizons and seen mothers come up to her with tears in their eyes, asking Temple to autograph their child's picture as they thank her for the book, *Emergence*, which helped each mom to understand what their silent child was thinking. People have stopped me in the ladies' room and asked, "What is she like?" Temple laughs, "What am I like? What does that mean?"

I have been fortunate enough to share private moments when she is sitting at an airport gate and needs a friend to talk to before the flight takes off. We ponder the plights of the world, such as the Iraq war or insurance coverage for her engineer and best friend, Mark. She described the Emmy awards as "a wild ride." She worries constantly about big picture issues such as education of today's youth: establishing boundaries, yet pushing each child just a little further than they thought they could go.

And when I hesitated with my career and considered bowing out, she told me, "Please don't, I need you. You have to warm the steel to bend it. We are making progress, even if it is just baby steps." So at the end of the day, I ask myself, why I am I part of Temple's inner circle? There are many that consider her special, and there are certainly those more educated, more renowned, and more revered. So it is with gratitude that I write this and say that being Temple's friend is a privilege, an honor, and a great responsibility. One that comes with expectation. She must find some reason for believing that the vision and goals she has are being carried out by those closest to her. So we all look with affection, respect, and appreciation. Thank you, Temple, for being our guide and our friend.

I met Helen at Temple's party, and have watched her in action out at the farm, where she was operating the hydraulic controls of the center track restrainer as the cattle were coming through. She's currently one of Temple's graduate students.

Here is what Helen said:

Helen C. Kline
Graduate Teaching/Research Assistant
Livestock Behavior and Welfare
Department of Animal Sciences
Colorado State University

Dr. Temple Grandin is a modern-day titan in both the autism and agricultural communities. When I first met her, as a freshman in college, I heard her speak at the George Bush Library at Texas A&M University.

She spoke about common agricultural practices and how her autism allows her to see the world in a different way. I walked away from that presentation with a passion to pursue new innovative ideas to benefit the agricultural industry, but also a new understanding of how my own little sister, who has autism, perceives the world. Dr. Grandin has given me the opportunity to explore my own potential as an animal science graduate student, while providing guidance for my own personal growth and development.

I also met Faith at CSU, and she's currently Temple's graduate student as well.

Faith Baier
Research/Teaching Assistant
Department of Animal Sciences
Livestock Behavior & Welfare
Colorado State University

Dr. Temple Grandin has impacted my life in many ways, and my journey with her has only begun. Earning the opportunity to work with Temple has been an amazing experience. Temple always shows her strong passion for the agriculture industry and mentoring others. She is incredibly dedicated to making a difference. Her strong desire to help and inform others is very inspiring. She always makes sure to be present for her class, even with a crazy travel schedule. She manages many speaking and professional events with ease. She never fails to amaze me with her many talents, passion for life and animals, and abundance of knowledge about nearly everything. She truly has defied numerous odds throughout her life. Her strong devotion to communicate how she views the world in pictures serves as a reminder for me to always remain observant. Oftentimes, problems with animals (and life in general) can be solved by paying attention to the simple details. There is no sense in making things more complicated than they truly are. Temple will forever impact how I think and view situations throughout my life. I am constantly inspired to reach for more and strive to leave an impact on the world, even if it's only a fraction of what she has already created.

Morgan is also one of Temple's current graduate students, whom I also met at CSU.

Morgan Schaeperkoetter

Graduate Teaching/Research Assistant

Department of Animal Sciences

Livestock Behavior and Welfare

Colorado State University

Since I was a young girl, I have always taken a special interest in animals. I asked my parents for many different types of animals, from when I was barely walking all the way through high school. I would always take special care for each animal, no matter how small or wild, including my passion for horses, cattle, and hogs as I was growing up.

I always felt a special connection to them, almost as if I could look at them and understand what they felt or needed. For many years I heard of Temple Grandin, the special way she interacted with animals, and the unique way in which she understood them. She became an advocate for the way they were handled, even as they were raised and transported to facilities to become food for the American consumer. I admired her and her role as a strong, influential woman in agriculture. I was so moved by how she didn't change or try to fit in, but stood out in the crowd and became a new voice for the industry.

Temple influenced my life profoundly. I felt a special connection to her over the years as I read her books and publications, and watched the movie that was made about her life. The first time I saw Temple in action was when I was working as an intern at Seaboard Foods, and looked over in the plant to see her working with the team, advising them on how hogs were being moved about in their processing facility. I had always been interested in going into this career, and as I learned more about how she helped facilities and the industry understand the need for humane animal handling, it became even more apparent that I wanted to learn from her and her passion for animals and the handling of them. She greatly influenced my career choice by bringing to the forefront of the industry the need to be an advocate for animals. She brought about a revolution of the importance of the industry's handling of animals as they become part of American agriculture's ability to feed the world, and ultimately gave my career choice even more purpose and meaning.

Today, as I work under Temple as one or her graduate students, I feel an unbelievable amount of drive and passion to make a positive impact on the industry just as she has. She took a chance on me, and accepts me just as I am. I never have to change who I am around Temple, she encourages me for my strengths and doesn't hold me down for my weaknesses. I plan to make her proud and utilize her mentorship as a driving force for my career in the animal agriculture industry.

Working at 100%

At Temple's seventieth birthday celebration, Temple got up to speak. It was there where, for the first time, Temple revealed that she has fully funded eighteen graduate students over the years; their entire tuition, and all expenses. This was very shocking to many, including myself. Later, after the party, I asked her about it. She told me that she uses all the money she earns going to speak to fund her students. I stated that I was extremely impressed, to which she replied, "It's a lot of money, but you can't take it with you. It's the right thing to do."

I asked Temple why is it important to her for her students to be published. Her answer logical and to the point. "Well, why bother to do research if you don't publish it? The whole purpose of research is to advance knowledge and make constructive change take place. It also helps their careers to be published." I then asked Temple what she does to help them achieve that goal. She replied, "When they write,

I immediately read it. In fact, in our department, there's a new rule. They can't graduate unless they get papers done and published. It's not enough to just do their thesis. They've got to do research and get it published."

One of Temple's graduate students talked at length to me about the research that she had done with pigs. She had gotten the paper published in a scientific journal prior to initiating contact with Temple. When she finally did meet her, Temple was very pleased that this student had the initiative to have already done that. In fact, when I was in Temple's vehicle as we drove back to CSU from the farm, I brought up that student to her. Temple was very enthusiastic about her because she had already done the research on the pigs and was published. Temple was very pleased indeed, stating that she knows that student will do extremely well with her career in the future. Like she said, that published article is that student's portfolio.

On the topic of the livestock industry, I asked "How do you feel as a highly successful female in a male dominated field?" Temple's reply was, "You've got to be twice as good and work three times harder than the guys. One of the things that was really appalling to me was that I was on projects that guys would really screw up, I'm talking millions of dollars' worth of screw ups, and they would still manage to have jobs afterward. In one instance, someone was building a meat packing plant that didn't have enough waste water treatment. It got shut down. They had been told by all the engineers that they didn't have enough waste water treatment, and the individual responsible for it still had his job after a screw up that big! That's ego. It overloaded the town's waste water treatment system. They were told they were going to overload the system. That's what's so stupid about the whole thing."

Temple continued, "The industry is less male-dominated now, so the females coming out of my program are getting great jobs. A lot of them are going into the animal welfare auditing companies; I've got two that have become professors, which is good. When I started in this field, there were no women in the live cattle part of it. The only place there would be females were in the offices as secretaries. You know, I totally agree where Sheryl Sandberg says that a man will take a job at a 60 percent level of competence, and a woman wants to be at 90 percent. When I did that dip vat project it was at the 60 percent level, and I said give me three weeks, because there was a lot on concrete reinforcement I didn't know. I figured it would take me at least ten days to lay my hands on the drawings showing how to do the concrete reinforcement for the dip vat. Back then, everything had to be done in the mail. Then I got up to 100 percent."

You do know who Sheryl Sandberg is, right?

As you can see, Temple's students think the world of her, and she maintains the highest of integrity at all times. This brings to my mind something Temple shared with me, an experience from her college days, regarding her view of a college professor that got shattered by his unprofessional behavior. Unfortunately, we see this all too often, and with social media it becomes rampant. It is really sad that the young people of today don't have the role models of days gone by. Temple is a rarity, as I can safely say she'll never make a cover of anything for some bad behavior.

Meeting the God of Psychology

One day I asked Temple, "Who were you most impressed meeting, who's the most famous person you've ever met?" I nearly fell off my chair with this one; she got pretty fired up recalling this event. Without hesitation, Temple blurted out, "I got to meet B.F. Skinner! I wrote him a letter about my squeeze machine. Then he wrote me back, saying what impressed him the most was the fact that I wrote to him, and that I was ambitious enough to do these projects. I was just a young college student so that was a huge deal, that B.F. Skinner answered the letter I sent him and invited me to come to his office. It was like having an audience with the Pope. I then asked Temple, "Tell me about the day you received his letter." Temple replied, "I was like, 'Oh my god! B.F. Skinner is willing to see me!' I was so excited holding that letter in my hand. I remembered that I went and shared the news with my psychology professor. I was a psychology major at that time. And it was relatively quickly when I went to see him from the time I got that letter. Maybe a few weeks."

"I remember when I went into that building and looked up, it was like the temple of psychology, and I was going to meet with the god of psychology! I can also remember going into his office and he had a plant that was growing all over the place. He was an older, gray-haired man, and he motioned to sit in a chair, so we were about four or five feet apart from each other. The old letch asked to touch my legs! I told him he may look at them, but he may not touch them. I had on a dress, a really conservative dress, and he wanted to touch my legs! Just recently I was telling someone about that whole thing, and they said, 'Oh, that was typical B.F. Skinner!' When I started reading all the stuff about Harvey Weinstein, it made me think of B.F. Skinner. Anyway, after I told him that, he backed off and never tried it again. I was alone with him in his office, in the daytime during business hours, at the Williams James Psychology building at Harvard. It was very quick into the conversation when he asked if he could touch my legs!"

Temple continued her story, "I can remember walking up to the William James building, which was a very impressive building. I can remember standing in front of the front door and looking at the size of the building, like it was the monument of psychology. I was going to the epicenter of psychology. Well, that's how I felt as I went into the William James building. I felt a little different coming out. Oh, and when I went to my car it had a ticket on it. I was pretty disappointed when he asked to touch my legs. I mean, he wrote all these psychology books, he was just on the cover of *Time* magazine. He instantly wasn't a god anymore, just a guy. Then I remember walking together to his rat colony, and I said to him, 'If only we could learn about the brain.' He said, 'We don't need to learn about the brain, we have operant conditioning. In fact, I've written about this in *Animals in Translation*.' Those were the things I remember we talked about the most. I guess I just thought everything would be more impressive, then I saw that it was just an ordinary office, with an ordinary-looking professor in it. The outside of the building was impressive, like ten stories tall. But that was it. And then, after he asked if he could touch my legs, he instantly was just a regular person, and not a god."

"I had another really creepy psychology professor like that when I was at Franklin Pierce College," she went on to say. "Yes," I commented, "it's really sad when someone of that magnitude does something like that to shatter their image and reputation."

Being a Good Role Model

Temple truly has a commanding sense of responsibility for maintaining the highest of integrity. I thought back to the evening of August 29, 2017 when I was in Temple's vehicle going over to Cheryl Miller's house for a small gathering after the big celebration. I was personally overwhelmed from the big birthday event, and I asked Temple how she feel about the party. I said, "Temple, tell me how you feel right now after experiencing all of that! People flew in from all over the country to be here for your seventieth birthday. How does it feel to have just experienced it?" Temple looked right at me with an extremely serious look on her face and said, "Anita, I have this strong sense of responsibility, because a lot of kids look up to me. I've got to make sure I don't do something wrong, like all these movie actors, and like Weinstein. A lot of people look up to me and I've always got to be at my best. People often ask me how I like getting all the attention at the airport and I say, 'It's a responsibility. I've always got to behave because I'm always on

Chapter 25

display.' The higher you get, the further you're going to fall if you mess up. It's my responsibility."

I felt extremely overwhelmed in that moment, and I told her how proud I was to know her, someone who does maintain that sense of responsibility. Temple went on, "At that party, they had that beer named after me, but I had to drive so I only had two sips. There's no way I want to risk getting a DWI, so I certainly wasn't going to drink that and then drive. If I was staying at a hotel I could have had more than two sips and then just walked up to my room. I certainly would never do anything crazy like drink and drive, and get arrested and have my picture on the front page of tomorrow's newspaper." I ask myself this one question: why can't others be like Temple?

CHAPTER 26
Temple's Big Message

During the many long conversations I had with Temple for the writing of this book, I asked her to share her biggest message that she wanted to convey. What was the most important thing to her? I already knew what she was going to say. "I want to convey something that's going to get those kids (those on the autism spectrum) out there doing something to be successful," she said. "There was a lot of stuff I did that was creative, where I had to figure out how to get in the back door for something. In the movie, they show that I went up to the editor to get their card. I actually did that. And you learned how to do that stuff too, and that's how you got to be successful. I think that's really important to convey. It's important to get out there and actually do things. Like when I got that press pass, that got me into a lot of really important meetings."

Sell Your Work by Having a Portfolio

Temple proceeded, "I also figured out that if you meet the right person, it can open a lot of doors. I learned early on that you need to have your portfolio readily available. I think today it's a lack of resourcefulness, maybe related to a lack of hands-on things. I think people just don't think of it. But they need to start thinking of alternative ways to get into things. I'm sure Bernie Rollins told you how I called him up when I wanted to get into Colorado State University. That's how I got in; Bernie helped me a lot. He helped get me tenure there, and I appreciate that."

Temple continued, "A lot of people just don't think to try and get in a back door. For example, I meet so many moms, and I'll ask them if they have any of their kid's artwork on their phone. They'll have maybe one piece, not even a good one. I tell them they need to get all the good stuff on the phone. Then it's like a portfolio! I think the fact that they took out a lot of the hands-on classes in school is a real problem. It took away a lot of the problem-solving opportunities. I learned to sew in school, then I took sewing classes at the sewing machine store. Then I got a job helping a seamstress, using my skills to sew. I didn't like the cooking classes at school!" Temple isn't joking about not liking her cooking classes. She doesn't even make coffee at home; nothing!

Teaching Work Skills

Temple still had more to say, "I recently had a teacher come up to me and tell me that they have a great program getting the non-verbal kids to talk. But then when they get older, they want to stay on their computers playing little games. She was affiliated with a big medical center in Boston, so they were doing great at early intervention, but dropped the ball on the transition to young adulthood and work. People need to limit the time these kids can be on the computer! It has to start at age eleven. Get them walking dogs, working at a church, volunteering at the old folk's home, or a food kitchen. Be a volunteer at many different things! Now what you don't want to do, is what I recently saw. A mother took her eighteen-year-old daughter, who lived a very sheltered life, and got her a job as a cashier in a busy clothing store at the holiday rush season. That was a mess. The girl got totally overwhelmed. I talked to that girl and her mom and said that was a big mistake. You need to get back on the horse, but that was a retail bucking bronco. You need to get on a gentler horse and do that store in the summertime. That's like throwing her in the deep end of a pool. You've got to start them out slowly. They must start learning how to do jobs outside the home! They have to wean them off the video games gradually. You can't do it suddenly, it has to be done gradually. But it needs to be done! I'm seeing so many kids graduating from high school, and they haven't learned one work skill. I want to get rid of the transition to work. The kids that are in the pipeline now need to start volunteer jobs at eleven, and the second they're legal age, get summer jobs and learn how to work. This is something that's a big part of my talk. I'm seeing two kinds of outcomes. Where the parents push the kid to get out there and do stuff, they are able to work and get jobs. On the other hand, the ones that let the kid stay on the video games, it's really bad." I chimed in, "Parents need to avoid letting the situation get to that point. It's up to them to get those kids out there doing stuff: socializing, and yes, making blunders—but they've got to do it." Temple replied, "Yes, they do!"

I knew Temple was on a roll here, as this is her favorite topic … even more than anything about NASA or astronauts. "I met this boy:

thirteen years old and fully verbal. He had never been in a store by himself to shop." I said, "There again, whose fault is that? The parent(s) can go in the store with the kid, but let him pick out the items and go to the register. They can be right behind him for safety purposes, but get him used to doing those tasks."

"That's exactly right," Temple replied.

"I think it's really important that I still have my career in the cattle industry. I see too many kids getting hung up on their autism diagnosis with that becoming their entire identity. I like to think about resourcefulness. In today's society, people don't make things. There's no resourcefulness. People will ask me things like how to find a good college for their kid. Well, you just get online and start searching for colleges that have programs for students with autism. Times have changed so much. I heard this story the other day about an eight-year-old boy who kicked the principal. They called the cops, and the kid ended up in court. When I was that age, I'd do bad things, and I'd get in trouble for it. Mother would have to come and pick me up from school and take me home. I'd have a giant meltdown. So once home, there would be no television that night."

Don't Get Stuck on Labels

"I'm seeing too many people getting that 'handicapped' mentality. I do believe there needs to be accommodations, but I think there's a point you can over-accommodate. It's getting to be too much medical model. All that medical model is just a bunch of gobbledygook!" (Did you know this is a real word in the dictionary? I started laughing when I heard Temple say it. To be sure I had the correct spelling, I looked it up.) Temple continued, "People are getting trapped in the mindset of the handicapped mentality. I can remember years ago at an autism conference meeting a mother and her son. He had just been diagnosed with autism or Asperger's, and had an IQ of 150 or 160. Back then, they called these kids gifted. Now, it's getting so much into the label that they can't even see what the kid can do. See, as a visual thinker, I don't see the label. This is especially a problem with the fully verbal kids, and it's gotten worse since they changed the Asperger's into the autism. It's made everything worse. The parents tend to over-protect, so the kid isn't learning anything."

"That's why I started talking about 'work-arounds' at my presentations. Working memory issues? You make a checklist that has a sequence in it. Temple continued, "Parents come up to me, and they're so hung up on diagnosis. I always have some basic trouble-shooting questions, and I'll use engineering terminology. Let's get down to basics on your kid's age. Is it a three-year-old where we're going to do standard intervention, or elementary school age, teenager, adult? Next, I need to know speech level. I need to get some idea where the kid is at. If they're at an age where they should be able to read, can they? At what level? What kind of problem are they having? If it's a kid over five, I need to have a lot of information—is it bullying, can't sit still, won't do their homework, can't stand the noise in the classroom? I need to know all this before I'll offer any advice." I replied, "Yes, obviously you need to gather all of this first."

Temple still had more to add, "Then, we talk about executive functioning. My speech teacher taught me executive functioning, it was called 'wait to take your turn' when we played the board game. She put a lot of emphasis on that. Stand in line and wait your turn, don't cut into the line, wait your turn. You had to learn to wait your turn!"

And more on the medical model, Temple added, "On the medical model, with the fully verbal kids, I think that's holding them back on the job front. However, a diagnosis is helpful for an older child, teenager, or adult to help them understand why they're having problems with relationships." As a person who didn't discover I'm on the autism spectrum until I was fifty, I couldn't agree more.

This truly is Temple's big message, her big dream for everyone on the autism spectrum: "The bottom line is, I want to see kids be successful. I want them to be able to get and keep jobs, to not get in trouble with the law, to not get into drugs, to get married and have a family, and to have a good life. I recently talked to two moms at a conference, one with a young daughter, the other a son. The girl had gotten a job for three summers in a row at the front counter of an ice cream shop. She had to wait on customers, scoop ice cream, serve it, and handle money. She became interested in nursing, and now is in college to become a nurse! She developed the necessary skills while working at that ice cream job. The boy, however, got hooked on video games, and the parents can't get him off them."

Chapter 26

Temple went on about experiences at conferences, "When a parent says they're 'thinking' about getting their kid a job, I tell them, 'Well you can't just think about it! You've got to just do it!' While academics are important, parents get too hung up on their kids' Individualized Education Program (IEP), and totally forget about the need to learn life skills. They get so focused on putting kids in advanced placement classes, that you've got kids in Silicon Valley jumping in front of a train due to the pressure they're under from overload of academics. When I was a kid, I'd make a lot of things and do experiments, but these kids of today, they're standing behind their mothers as the mother is doing all the talking for them. When I was their age, I was already shopping for snacks on my own in a grocery store! I was also attracted to doing authoritative things, like working the cattle and operating the hydraulic chute. I'd have to push until I got to do it. I loved to bring up the cattle, but I got really excited when I got to operate the hydraulic squeeze chute. Once the crew working with the cattle saw that I could do it, they eased up on me. I always had to prove myself. I can remember the first feed yards I ever went to: I watched, and watched, and watched. Then, I just picked up one of the vaccinating guns and I started vaccinating the cattle! (Temple sounded quite pleased with herself.) I can still remember the day I did that."

I was curious, trying to envision the reactions those men would have had toward a stranger—even worse, a female stranger—who just came in and started working. "Temple," I asked, "at these feed lots, what were the worker's reactions to you?" She gushed proudly, "They usually just let me do it! They were probably shocked. Then, when everyone would take a break, they'd come over and talk to me. They'd accept me for the most part. The ones who gave me the most trouble about being a girl were the foremen. And it wasn't the big bosses, it was always middle management. Discrimination. Once I had to tell the foreman that the corrals didn't work, and he responded by slapping me on the butt. Now that's a very difficult thing to have to deal with." I was wondering about things like that happening to a lone female at those big cattle ranches with tons of men there.

Temple started, "I'm on my bed here in my hotel room, and I've got this big stack of my books piled up next to me. I've got to sign all of them for the conference. I'm trying really hard not to get any marker on this white bedspread!"

"Oh, that's too funny!" I replied. "I'm just picturing you like that! What a great scene for this book, for everyone to envision."

Let me also share this with you, a new phenomenon Temple is noticing at conferences. She exclaimed, "Let me tell you what else I'm seeing! At these conferences, I'm seeing all kinds of people my age coming up to me to tell me they just found out their grandkid is on the spectrum, and once they learn about it, they're pretty sure they're on the autism spectrum, too! I just got a letter from an eighty-one-year-old. He said he saw my movie, and really resonated with it. He then understood why he was the way he was! These are people that had decent jobs their whole life; they were in IT, accounting, or and other professions, and they only found out about their ASD when

Chapter 26

their grandkid got diagnosed! They never knew why they didn't fit in, but they all had decent jobs. A man around the age of sixty recently came up to me to say his granddaughter just got diagnosed, and he realized that he has autism. That helped him understand himself. I'm really starting to think that the fully verbal kids, who can read and write at an adult level, are being held back by their autism diagnosis. What I'm learning from these older people who discovered they were on the spectrum later in life is that their diagnosis helped with their relationships."

Temple had more to say, "Since they changed the Diagnostic and Statistical Manual of Mental Disorders, Fifth Edition (DSM-5) in 2013, it seems to have gotten worse. There are instances of kids who are seventeen, eighteen, even nineteen years old who have never shopped. The difference between these kids and the previous generation is that the older people had jobs when they were kids! I was at an airport the other day and I saw an article in a magazine about the kids of today, how they're not learning how to work. This had nothing to do with autism! It was about kids in general."

Let me tell you about what Temple experienced the other day at an autism conference. "I was in McGowan, Texas the other day, and a family came up to me and said the advice I'd given them two years earlier was life changing. I asked, what advice did I give you? They said, 'You told us to get our ASD kid out and actively doing things! We did that, and it's been life changing.' This was an elementary school age kid, fully verbal. Remember when I talked about Mr. Patey at the boarding school, who refused to allow me to become a recluse at the school? That's the only way to get these kids going!"

This really upsets Temple. "These kids of today make their autism their identity. You've got to work really hard with early intervention to get little kids talking. After that, these kids need to be out in the world doing things, like joining the Girls Scouts or Boy Scouts, or doing some kind of job to teach them career skills."

That was Temple's big message she wanted to get out there. I think she said it loud and clear. To all who are on the autism spectrum, don't look at your autism diagnosis! When you take your eyes off the goal and look at your autism, you are the one creating your own obstacles. Instead, look ahead at whatever goal you choose and work diligently towards achieving it. Never take your eyes off that goal!

CHAPTER 27
Being Different— Really Different!

ometimes I'd call Temple and she would start telling me about a lengthy conversation she had with someone, like perhaps a young adult with autism, who got her phone number and simply called her to ask for advice. Once, she had just finished up a call from a young male on the spectrum who was asking advice on how to deal with anger. Temple told him she learned how to control her anger by learning how to cry. I asked her when that happened, and she told me, "I got in a gigantic fist fight at my boarding school. They took away horseback riding for two weeks. That's when I switched! I was still miserable, but that was the end of the fighting. The fight ensued because I was being bullied and being called names by a boy at school. He kept at it, and finally I punched him—with both fists. I had to learn that you just don't do that. He got in some trouble, but I got in a lot more trouble. I told the boy on the phone about a time when I was younger. I was at a job, and I had a plant manager screaming the obscenities at me for four hours straight during an equipment startup. I'd go to the engine room and cry to vent my anger. I'd just go cry! You can't ever show any signs of anger at any job. Never. I also explained to him that at seventeen, I was cleaning out horse stalls and hand-painting signs! I wasn't giving autism talks."

Here's what I mean about Temple being different from others who are different. Temple is a global phenomenon, but you'd never know it by how humble she is. She answers the phone for anyone who calls her hoping to talk to her. No one at her level of fame does that. They simply don't. She's not arrogant or conceited, she treats everyone with the same respect. She doesn't live in a million-dollar home. Instead, she uses her money for very philanthropic purposes, and chooses to live a modest lifestyle.

I asked Temple the following question for your sake. As for myself, I wouldn't have had to ask it, as I knew what her answer would be. "Temple, do you have any regrets in your life? She answered, "Well, I've done a lot of exciting things. Yes, there are some things I didn't do, that others have. But I've experienced many great things. I was just out to dinner with someone and I was showing them pictures of my trip to Cape Kennedy, and they said, 'Boy, you sure have an exciting life, and get to do exciting things!' Sure, there's things in life that I don't have that other people have, but I've done a lot of really unique things. I don't regret anything." I replied, "Indeed, you have."

I hope you feel like you have gotten to know Temple Grandin like you never thought possible. I've shared every last detail of her life with you, so she's like your new friend. In fact, I'd bet you know more about Temple now than you do about your best friend! I hope you realized that Temple is, mostly, just like everyone else. What do I mean by that? Well, here's the deal: on one hand Temple is just like everyone else, but she has massive perseverance, ethics, and that sense of responsibility far beyond the average Joe. Temple truly is "all that and a bag of chips!"

I've just got to tell you this one last thing that happened, because I think you will see it to be as profound as I did. After her seventieth birthday celebration, Temple and I were in her vehicle driving over to Cheryl Miller's home for a private party. I asked Temple, "Don't you feel proud of yourself for all your accomplishments?" She went on, "Of course I'm proud of myself, but I've never let that get to my head. I feel good doing the right thing!" I felt totally overwhelmed at that moment, realizing that I'm sitting there in a vehicle with one of the most famous people in the world, and she just said that. That was one of the most profound moments of my life. I will remember it forever. Temple Grandin truly is one of the most influential people of our time.

■ AFTERWORD ■

Wow, this has been quite the journey. On that rainy day when Temple called me at work, I couldn't have known what would evolve from that conversation. It evolved into one of my most critical missions of my life. Temple's great sense of responsibility has osmosed into me: I felt it my duty to enable you to get to know her like she's your new best friend, and I am using this book as a megaphone to blast Temple's big message to the millions of individuals on the autism spectrum.

This also became a very personal journey for myself. As Temple and I talked, we learned more and more about each other. I discovered how very much I am like Temple. Temple wanted me to tell you everything, in particular about the fact that I came from a very poor family. Do you remember back in Chapter 13, where Temple shared things that make her cry? People have bashed her because she came from a wealthy family; they've said that's the reason why Temple got to where she is. After reading this book, you should know that Temple got to where she is due to her extreme perseverance, thirst for knowledge, and endless hard work. So, why does Temple want me to tell you that I came from a very poor family? She wants people to see that an individual with autism who comes from a poor family can become successful by those same virtues: extreme perseverance, a thirst for knowledge, and endless hard work. Yes, it sure can be done. It isn't easy, but it can be done.

Temple also knows of all the childhood jobs I did, jobs that built the foundation for my future. I've been working since I was twelve years old. There was no such thing as having to 'transition' from high school or college to the work world; it evolved over time, a gradual progression, gaining strength and momentum as I went along.

Like Temple, I spent a lot of my youth mucking out horse stalls and being in charge of school horses and the barn. I started that job when I was twelve and worked every summer, as well as weekends and holidays, into my early twenties. Temple did all those same things while she was at the boarding school. There were many other jobs we both did as kids, which got us out there "doing stuff," as Temple likes to say! Each job was yet another learning experience of learning life skills. There's no substitute for this path to success. The only way to get there is by starting at a very early age to start doing some kind of job or volunteer work, and experiencing anything that gets you out interacting with others and learning new things. A person can't sit home on their computer, get a degree, then think you can go out and then learn how to work. Autism or not, it's up to the parents to get these kids active and engaged. Temple told me about an article she read in some business magazine while she was at an airport just recently. It was about the kids of today not knowing how to work. It wasn't about kids with autism, just kids in general. Well, it's a sign of our time. Parents let their kids get addicted to video games and all kinds of electronics, and spend all their time on them. I never see kids outside playing hopscotch, tag, or any other old-fashioned kid games. Nor are they out doing any sort of jobs.

Afterword

Today, kids with autism are the ones struggling because they didn't get started young doing what Temple and I did: working. We came from a generation where hard work was just the normal way of life. There were no computers, no video games, no tablets, nothing to sit and interact with in solitude day after day, accomplishing nothing. We all had paper routes, worked around the home, helped out on the farm, and learned to work and accrue life skills.

I hope the pages within this book serve to change the world's view of autism. I have left no stone unturned in revealing the depth of Temple Grandin. The world got a great look at her life in the HBO movie *Temple Grandin*, and I have now taken you on a longer journey to know her.

As for my own personal journey on this endeavor, I have gained strength I never knew I had. In my long conversations with Temple, I could see and feel her courage and strength, and it empowered me. It's just like Dorothy and her red ruby slippers: she discovered that when she clicked them together, they took her home. She had the power all along, but she just didn't know it. I had the power all along, too, only I didn't know it until Temple showed me the door to open it. Let this book of her life show you the door, too.

SPECIAL THANKS

My biggest thanks go to Temple Grandin, for taking the time out of her extremely demanding schedule to have our long talks that made this book possible. Also, for patiently answering my endless questions, often about things that brought up significant memories and emotions. Temple is a visual thinker, like myself. This enabled her to simply pull up every single memory of her entire life at the drop of a hat. No matter what I asked, she'd instantly be able to answer my question as if it occurred only an hour earlier.

If it weren't for Teresa Corey, this book wouldn't have happened. I give my forever gratitude to her for that.

It isn't every day that you get to talk to an Emmy Award-winning Hollywood Director. My deepest thanks to Mick Jackson for our long talk, and for writing the foreword for this book.

Cheryl Miller was instrumental in numerous things regarding the production of this book. I give endless thanks for all that.

Thank you to Jennifer Gilpin Yacio, for believing in me to carry out this mission;

Rose Heredia-Bechtel, for her endless patience and encouragement;

Morgan Nonamaker, for her ultra-speedy copy editing and perfectly keeping my writing style;

Jim Uhl, Temple's great friend and business partner;

Mark, Temple's great friend;

Rosalie Winard, Temple's great friend;

Erika Voogd, Temple's great friend;

Dr. Bernard Rollins, Colorado State University Professor;

Temple's former students Kurt Vogel, PhD and Ruth Woiwode, PhD; and

Temple's Graduate Students—Dana Wagner, Miriam Martin, Faith Baier, Morgan Schaeperkotter, Helen Kline.

I continued to work full-time during this entire book project. I'm up at three o'clock in the morning and in the operating room by five in the morning each weekday. The next nine hours are spent in the fast-paced, high-stress operating room doing general anesthesia for surgery. While there, I have to listen to heavy metal or some kind of angry music, which physically drains me. I've recently discovered that the loud music I'm subjected to all day stimulates my sympathetic nervous system. This is the body's fight or flight defense mechanism. Because it's constantly bombarded, I'm physically wiped out by three in the afternoon, when I typically get out of work. I also have mitochondrial dysfunction, meaning my mitochondria are only functioning at 60 percent. With the addition of having to interact with surgeons, operating

Special Thanks

room staff, and patients all day, I'm at rock bottom on energy by the time I get home.

This book had to get done. The only way that could happen was with all the help from my husband, Abraham, who also has autism. He works full time, too, but at his job he's in peace and quiet at his desk, creating the blueprint drawings all day. Abraham kept the household going: laundry, cooking, cleaning, tending to all our animals, and tending to me. Totaling up all the conversations I had with Temple and everyone else, I had over sixty hours of recordings to transcribe and put it all together. He did a great job of keeping me calm, and reading my work aloud for me so I can hear how it sounds. We did it as a team. I'd be at the kitchen table writing, as he would be assembling our lunches for the next day, and gathering everything to be ready for our breakfast shake the next morning. He'd make me fresh-squeezed limeade to sip as I wrote, and steam me a head of cauliflower to snack on. He did whatever it took to keep me going to get this book done, and without him, I couldn't have done it. Thank you, my love, as always and forever.

■ ABOUT THE AUTHOR ■

Anita Lesko, BSN, RN, MS, CRNA

Anita is an internationally recognized autism advocate and member of Autism Society of America's Panel of Autistic Advisors. She was recently diagnosed with Asperger's Syndrome at the age of fifty. She graduated from Columbia University in New York City with a master of science degree in Nurse Anesthesia in 1988, and has been working full-time ever since as an anesthetist, specializing in anesthesia for neurosurgery. Anita is honored to have been a speaker at the United Nations Headquarters for World Autism Awareness Day 2017.

Her husband, Abraham, also has autism. They opened their wedding to the public to show that individuals with autism have a need for love, relationships, and marriage just like everyone else. The event attracted international media attention, including *People* and *Good Morning America.*

She is a contributing author for numerous publications including the *Autism Asperger's Digest* and *The Mighty.* She is a blogger for the International Board of Credentialing and Continuing Education Standards. Anita's first book, *Asperger's Syndrome: When Life Hands You Lemons, Make Lemonade,* a memoir, was written immediately after she was diagnosed. She co-authored her second book, *Been There. Done That. Try This! The Aspie's Guide to Life on Earth,* with Dr. Tony Attwood and Craig Evans.

Anita is a Project Co-Lead on a $250,000 PCORI-funded grant for Adults with Autism and other Stakeholders Engaging Together. This project aims to improve health and health care for adults with autism. Anita is on a mission to enable everyone with autism around the world to receive the best healthcare. She combined her autism and thirty years' experience as a medical professional to write the book The Complete Guide to Autism & Healthcare to reach this goal. She sees the need to educate all health care providers about autism and how to best communicate with individuals on the spectrum, enabling providers to provide quality care to this rapidly growing population.

Henry Ford, founder of the Ford Motor Company (also known as an American captain of industry) had a quote, "Obstacles are those frightful things you see when you take your eyes off your goal." Unbeknownst to her, Anita has been living by this rule throughout her entire life. Only recently did she hear this quote from Temple during their many conversations. Throughout those first fifty years when Anita didn't know she was on the autism spectrum, she didn't understand why she was so different and never fit in. Despite all the sensory and social challenges, she never took her eyes off her goal, whatever it was.

During the many long conversations with Temple Grandin for the production of this book, Anita discovered how much they have in common. Anita's successful career as a Certified Registered Nurse Anesthetist puts her in a fast-paced, high-stress environment with massive sensory input, which is not easy for someone on the autism spectrum to function in. Anita attributes her ability to work in this arena to her numerous childhood jobs—many of the same that Temple had. Anita came from a very poor family, and when she wanted something she had to work very hard to get it. All throughout high school, Anita worked every weekend and summer at a big stable where she mucked out endless stalls. Her duties evolved to caring for the school horses, the lesson program, and the numerous chores that went along with it. Of course, she was riding every opportunity she got, and rode in shows jumping horses over six-foot-high fences. Being a working student was extremely hard work, but she reached her riding goals with that opportunity.

Other jobs she did in her teen years and early adulthood included a variety of tasks, all of which set the foundation for building interpersonal social skills and learning how to work. Each job brought new skills to learn, which ultimately enabled her to work as an anesthetist. Some of those early jobs included working as a skate guard and at the concession stand at a public ice skating arena. Each of those necessitated interacting with people, much like Temple tending to all the guests at her mother's dinner parties. During some of the shows, Anita operated the spotlights, which were located high above the arena floor on a platform; Temple had also operated spotlights like that when she was the same age! Anita learned to sew, cook, and bake from her mom, and Temple had a job sewing in her teens. Anita worked throughout undergraduate school as a graphic arts designer for the college, which contributed to her receiving the awards Who's Who Among Students in American Colleges & Universities in 1982 and 1983.

Temple was extremely impressed that Anita accumulated over one hundred thousand dollars in student loans for her master's degree and paid it all back over a ten-year period. Temple feels that Anita is proof that a person with autism coming from a poor family can become successful through hard work and perseverance.

Anita continues working full time as an anesthetist while working tirelessly as an autism advocate. Her ultimate goal is to change the world's view of autism, enabling all on the autism spectrum to lead happier, more productive lives.

Photo courtesy of Anita Lesko

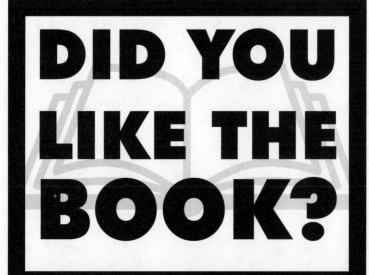